DAVID ROBERTS
TRAVELS IN EGYPT & THE HOLY LAND

DAVID ROBERTS
TRAVELS IN EGYPT & THE HOLY LAND

Debra N. Mancoff

In Association with the Library of Congress

Pomegranate

SAN FRANCISCO

Published by Pomegranate Communications, Inc.
Box 6099, Rohnert Park, CA 94917
(800) 227-1428; (707) 586-5500; www.pomegranate.com

Pomegranate Europe Ltd.
Fullbridge House, Fullbridge
Maldon, Essex CM9 4LE, England

Pomegranate Catalog No. A558

Library of Congress Cataloging-in-Publication Data

Mancoff, Debra N., 1950–
    David Roberts : travels in Egypt and the Holy Land / Debra N.
  Mancoff ; preface by Katherine L. Blood.
       p.   cm.
    Includes bibliographical references.
    ISBN 0-7649-1029-9 (pbk.)
    1. Roberts, David, 1796–1864.   2. Roberts, David, 1796–1864—
  Journeys—Egypt.   3. Roberts, David, 1796–1864—Journeys—
  Palestine.   4. Egypt—In art.   5. Palestine—In art.   6. Artists—
  Scotland Biography.
  I. Roberts, David, 1796–1864.   II. Title.
  NC242.R575M36   1999
  769.92—dc21
  [B]   99-26457
                                                                 CIP

Interior design by Poulson/Gluck Design

Printed in China

08 07 06 05 04 03 02 01 00 99   10 9 8 7 6 5 4 3 2 1

Frontispiece: John Ballantine, *David Roberts in His Studio*, c. 1866.
Fine Art Society, courtesy of Bridgeman Art Library, London.

Preface

By Katherine L. Blood

Assistant Curator, Fine Prints, Library of Congress

From a distance of 160 years, David Roberts's images of the Middle East continue to enthrall new audiences. Roberts made his first sketches of Egypt and the Holy Land in 1838 and 1839, just prior to major advances in photography and travel. The European art market of the day supported a host of genres aimed at extending the geographical and spiritual scope of the viewer, including sublime landscapes, religious spectacles, topographical views, and subjects related to the Orient and classical antiquity. Roberts invoked all of these in his series *The Holy Land, Syria, Idumea, Arabia, Egypt, and Nubia* (held in the Prints and Photographs Division of the Library of Congress). In doing so, he struck a balance between reportage and romanticism that has traveled well from Victorian galleries and living rooms to modern ones.

At the end of his eleven-month journey in the Middle East, Roberts returned to London with a trove of studies and sketches that would be the seeds for his most ambitious work to date. Having already gained solid success as a theatrical scene painter and landscape artist, Roberts knew his intended audience and the contemporary mechanisms for reaching them. Paintings were the common currency in formal, sanctioning venues such as the Royal Academy in London; Roberts exhibited his first group of Eastern oils at the Academy in 1840. His subjects included *The Greek church of the Holy Nativity at Bethlehem; The gate and Mosque of Mtuawellee, Grand Cairo; The Dromos, or outer court of the Great Temple of Edfou, In Upper Egypt; Statues of the Vocal Memnon in the plain of Thebes;* and *Remains of the portico of the Lesser Temple at Baalbec.* In the following year, he rose from Associate of the Royal Academy to full Academician.

For the widest dissemination of his work, however, Roberts envisioned an opulent folio publication to be sold by subscription. The printmaking technique of lithography had become the *lingua franca* for printed "views," continuing a thriving trade pioneered by aquatint topography in the eighteenth century. Made by drawing directly on a thick stone block with a greasy ink, lithography offered a cost-efficient vehicle for the distribution of images. The sturdiness of the stone matrix made it possible to print large editions, and a serial publication was likely to bring Roberts his greatest popular and commercial success. He set out to produce a folio of unparalleled splendor. After a flurry of offers and counteroffers, the search for the right publisher ended with Francis Graham Moon. As quoted by biographer Katherine Sim, Roberts detailed the terms of their arrangement and Moon's success in generating excitement for the project:

> When having been much importuned by Mr Moon I told him the circumstances connected with it, when he at once offered to bring it out in the manner I proposed viz. Two Vols on Syria, 130 subjects, price £21.00, Two Vols on Egypt Ditto, and one Vol: on modern Cairo, 60 subjects, price £10.10.0 making in all £52.10 and agreeing to pay me for the use of the same £3000. This was a great risk, I must confess, at such a price but by his Exhibiting the Drawings not only in London but almost every provincial

Town of any consequence, his *subscription* now [May 1840] is nearly double Murray's estimate. It must be admitted no other man but Moon could have effected it; what gratified me more perhaps than anything else was the subscription of my native Town, £1,700, which, for Edinburgh, was greater than even London itself in proportion to the wealth population of each.

Luster was added to the enterprise by such "celebrity" subscribers as Charles Dickens and the young Queen Victoria, to whom Roberts would dedicate the christening volumes.

The work of translating Roberts's original designs to stone was entrusted to watercolorist and lithographer Louis Haghe, of the prominent lithographic firm Day & Haghe. The collaboration between Moon, Roberts, and Haghe gave birth to a lavish forty-part publication that is still held by print scholars to be the most ambitious lithographic-plate book ever produced. Lithography historian Michael Twyman has written that with few exceptions " . . . it marks the last link between the established artist and topographical lithography." The final work consisted of 247 large-format lithographs by Haghe, based on Roberts's watercolors. The Reverend George Croly and William Brockedon were commissioned to write authoritative texts to accompany the lithographs. Croly was a well-known writer and critic, and a frequent contributor to leading journals of the day. Brockedon was a painter, inventor, and travel writer and illustrator. Both authors relied heavily on excerpts from Roberts's lively journal; Croly punctuated his descriptions with quotations from biblical scripture.

Against the vogue for sensational effects of scale, light, and shadow to intensify religious imagery (a technique he himself had used in previous work), Roberts grounded his compositions in the language of documentary topography, with the primary goal of showing the physicality of terrain and architecture. People were portrayed in the course of their daily business or at worship in mosques and churches, underscoring both the immediacy and the otherworldly romanticism of the scenes. Roberts chose to bathe his scenes in almost uniform brilliance. The luminous effect was carried forward by Haghe's use of tinted lithography, which involved building images in layers with overall background tints in warm, pale tones and the basic linear framework drawn in shades of black. White highlights were added by blocking out or scraping back areas of the tint stones. Finally, the lithographs were available to subscribers with or without additional hand coloring, which brought up details of visual emphasis and ornament.

Acclaim for Roberts's *Holy Land* drawings, paintings, and lithographs was widespread and effusive. One of the few ambivalent reactions came from the premier Victorian art and literary critic John Ruskin. In *Modern Painters,* Ruskin tempered his criticism of Roberts with this praise:

> The fidelity of intention and honesty of system of Roberts have, however, always been meritorious; his drawing of architecture is dependent on no unintelligible lines or blots, or substituted types; the main lines of the real design are always there, and its hollowness and undercuttings given with exquisite feeling; his sense of solidity of form is very peculiar, leading him to dwell

with great delight on the roundings of edges and angles; his execution is dexterous and delicate, singularly so in oil, and his sense of chiaroscuro refined.

Ironically, it was on the issue of visual fidelity that Ruskin took exception to Roberts's *Holy Land* drawings. He wrote: " . . . it is bitterly to be regretted that the accuracy and elegance of his work should not be aided by that genuineness of hue and effect which can only be given by the uncompromising effort to paint, not a fine picture, but an impressive and known *verity*."

Nevertheless, the press was overwhelmingly favorable about the series, and critics lined up to rhapsodize over the aesthetic quality of the work, its historical and topographical accuracy, and the grandeur of its subject matter. The prominent London journal *Art-Union* enthused:

> It is impossible to adequately describe the beauties of this work in all its departments. The execution and printing of the lithography places us, in this particular style, at the head of the list of Nations that value and cultivate Art . . . Coming before the world with the highest claims to consideration, as well in respect of its literary, as of its pictorial department, this work cannot be considered as of that mere temporary interest which is begotten of novelty; but must remain a GREAT STANDARD WORK of reference in all questions concerning the subject-matter of which it is constituted. It sets before us as facts of yesterday, the events

described in the New Testament; and illustrates the invincible truths of the Old.

These words proved to be prophetic. For nineteenth-century viewers, *The Holy Land, Syria, Idumea, Arabia, Egypt, and Nubia* was an artistic and cultural tour de force, functioning simultaneously as edifying art, devotional object, visual evidence, and exotica. The allure of this mixture has been amplified as the world Roberts recorded has become as removed in time as it was literally out of reach for most viewers of his day. The images created by Roberts and Haghe continue to engage modern scholars and collectors through the richness of their content and by the strength of their technique and artistry.

Author Debra N. Mancoff gives us an opportunity to travel with Roberts on his extraordinary journey through Egypt and the Holy Land. She is an ideal tour guide, framing Roberts's visual narrative with scholarly insight and a storyteller's gift for taking us back through time and full circle to the artist's central intention—that we sit back and take in the view.

ACKNOWLEDGMENTS

In writing this book, I enjoyed the support and assistance of many who willingly shared their time and expertise, and I'm glad for the opportunity to thank them. At Pomegranate, I especially thank Thomas F. Burke, for suggesting that I undertake this project, and Katie Burke, for sharing my interest and enthusiasm every step of the way. Without their encouragement, this book would not have been written. I would also like to thank James Donnelly and Zipporah W. Collins for their editorial guidance, and Poulson/Gluck Design for their fine work in turning my manuscript into a book.

A special debt of gratitude goes to the Publishing Office of the Library of Congress in Washington, D.C., most notably W. Ralph Eubanks, Director of Publishing, and Blaine Marshall, whose congenial help during my research visit—and many times after—was invaluable. Thanks also to Maja Keech, reference specialist, and the staff members of the Prints and Photographs Division for their assistance.

The Newberry Library of Chicago provided strong support. I thank the Department of Research and Education for giving me study space and access to the collections as a Scholar in Residence during the course of this project. The paging staff in Special Collections, including Julie Cobb, Christine Coburn, Aaron Fagan, David Senior, and Bart Lind Smith, with their constant good humor and enthusiastic interest, made using the collection a pleasure. I also want to thank Susan Summerfield of the Reading Room for her help.

At every stage in the project, colleagues demonstrated their willingness to listen, advise, and exchange ideas. For suggesting readings I would not have found on my own, I want to thank Kirsten Buick of the Art Institute of Chicago, William Vaughan of Birkbeck College, the University of London, and Phil Freshman. My appreciation also goes to Robert Warde of Macalester College and Joseph Berton for always being ready to answer questions and share their expertise. A special debt of gratitude goes to Mary Woolever, Archivist of the Ryerson and Burnham Archive of the Art Institute of Chicago, who happily exchanged ideas and information about "Egyptomania" in Europe and America, based on the research she did, with the assistance of Heather Oblak and Barbara Korbel, Conservator of the Ryerson and Burnham Library, for an exhibition held at the Art Institute of Chicago January–March 1998. And a special thank you to Roland Hansen, Readers' Services Librarian in the Flaxman Library at the School of the Art Institute of Chicago, for helping me find the books I needed.

Finally, I would like to recognize the people whose special support gave a deeper meaning to the project. I am very grateful to Mrs. Philippa Hunter Johnston, the great-great-granddaughter of David Roberts, for corresponding with me and sharing family reminiscences. Gratitude as well goes to my parents, Elinor R. Mancoff and Philip Mancoff, who assisted in this project in ways I could hardly have imagined. I would like to thank Caroline Kenny for her hospitality during my research trips in London. This book was written in memory of her mother, Lady Elizabeth Arthur (1 May 1906–12 April 1994), who always gave me a warm welcome when I was far from home.

D. N. M.
December 1998

INTRODUCTION

Late in the summer of 1838, British travel artist David Roberts (1796–1864) left London for the journey of his lifetime—a trip that would change how Europeans viewed the Middle East. Since boyhood, Roberts had dreamed of exploring the ancient lands of that region, a desire sparked by Bible stories and nourished with dramatic tales of the exotic Orient. Now, with his career as a painter on the rise, Roberts planned a journey to Egypt and the Holy Land. At long last he would satisfy his curiosity, but his expedition had a more ambitious goal. Roberts was determined to keep an accurate and vivid visual record of the sights he saw. Through his art he would bring the wonders of the Middle East to his audience at home.

Roberts embarked on his journey with little more than determination and confidence in his own artistic skill. He did not speak the languages of the region, and his knowledge of the area was gleaned more from popular publications than from scientific study. To pay for his trip, he drained his own finances. And he undertook the adventure alone, breaking the longstanding British tradition of artists traveling as members of a wealthy patron's entourage. Experience had taught him to rely upon his ability and his intuition; he was not afraid of risk if it would lead him to artistic achievement.

Born into humble circumstances in a rural town outside Edinburgh, Roberts had learned to trust his talent and his dreams. As a boy, he stretched his narrow horizons, walking from his village to the city to see the circus caravans and theatrical troupes that camped on the Earthen Mound. Family poverty kept him from formal art studies, but natural talent and ambition propelled him from an apprenticeship to a house painter, through a series of jobs as a theatrical set designer, to a successful career as a landscape painter in London. His work as a view painter won him his greatest acclaim and gave him his deepest satisfaction, fulfilling his wanderlust and drawing upon his ability to create a scene that would ignite the interest of his audience.

In choosing Egypt and the Holy Land as his destinations, Roberts reflected the enduring fascination of Western European culture with the ancient Middle East. For centuries, Europeans looked to the Middle East as the realm of the Bible, a place for veneration and pilgrimage. But the journey to these lands remained a rare and arduous undertaking, completed only by the deeply pious or the most intrepid traveler. At the turn of the nineteenth century, as the science of archaeology was rising, teams of scholars set out to map and measure the region, seeking to understand history through the analysis of ancient ruins and artifacts. Yet the myth of the Orient—as a strange and sensuous land—colored the perceptions of the region by people at home. To the modern European mind, the Middle East was as much a land of fable as of fact; this romantic view prevailed even in the light of scientific discovery.

Roberts made his journey at this crucial juncture of scientific observation and romantic fascination. He set out with little, but he returned with a bounty of sketches and a portfolio he described as "the most interesting that has ever left the country." The first British artist to explore the Middle East, Roberts presented his views of the region in the monumental volumes *The Holy Land, Syria, Idumea, Arabia, Egypt, and Nubia,* published in series during the years 1842 to 1849. In hand-tinted lithographs based on his designs and produced to his specifications, Roberts created a new vision of the Orient for the British public. Keenly observed and minutely detailed, his images made the region more tangible and accessible than ever before. In approaching accuracy, Roberts lost nothing of romanticism; like a skilled set designer, he used light, color, and atmosphere to stage a spectacle that convinced as it captivated, evoking an aura of exoticism as part of his realistic view. For the remainder of the century, British artists and tourists, inspired by Roberts's adventure, set out on their own expeditions to Egypt and the Holy Land, while armchair travelers, paging through the lithographs, thrilled to the journey in the comforts of home. In fulfilling his lifetime dream, David Roberts made the distant region his own realm, forever changing the way his countrymen viewed that part of the world.

Plate 0:1   Unknown artist. *Portrait of David Roberts.*
National Portrait Gallery, London.

DAVID ROBERTS WAS BORN IN the small village of Stockbridge near Edinburgh on 24 October 1796. His father, John, worked as a cobbler, his bench installed in the kitchen of the family's two-room tenement home. To supplement the father's modest income—limited by the small population of the village—the mother, Christina, occasionally took in laundry. David was the eldest child of five; he had two sisters and two brothers, but only his sister Lucy, born two years after him, survived childhood. The loss of his siblings—John at age ten, Alexander at seven, and Christine at only two—cast a shadow over his youth, and he would long remember "the heavy expenses attending their illness and death [that] caused my father to work with a heavy heart almost unceasingly night and day."

Like most boys of the poor working class, Roberts was expected to follow his father's trade. But his parents sought to educate him as well as their straitened circumstances would allow. Around the age of seven he attended a home school run by an elderly local woman, but he later believed that his time there was spent "more to keep me out of the way of being run over by carts or drowned in the Water of Leith than for anything she would or could

Chapter 1

DESTINED FOR A WANDERING LIFE

teach me." The following year, he was briefly enrolled in a day school in Edinburgh, where he endured whippings as part of the regular discipline. At first his father silenced his complaints, ordering him to respect his master, but, when Roberts repeatedly came home with the skin of his fingers flayed and his legs covered with welts, his education ended. John and Christina decided that their son would fare better as an apprentice.

Roberts showed little inclination for his father's trade, however. His interest was in drawing, and at an early age he could copy any picture set before him, earning him the nickname "the Natural Genius." His family owned a few cheap picture books of traditional tales such as *The Life and Death of Cock Robin* and *Little Red Riding Hood*. He also liked to wander off on his own, looking for subjects to draw. Often, Roberts would make the long walk into Edinburgh to visit the Earthen Mound, where he was intrigued by the brightly decorated caravans that transported traveling circuses and strolling players. He particularly loved the cloth banners that advertised exotic attractions: artists from distant lands and wild-beast shows. When he returned home from these excursions, his indulgent mother would allow him to recreate

Plate 1:1   Robert Scott Lauder, *Portrait of Roberts as a Young Man*, c. 1820.
Oil on canvas, 12 1/4 x 9 in. (31.1 x 22.9 cm). Scottish National Portrait Gallery, Edinburgh.

what he had seen on her kitchen walls with a red chalk known as *keel* and the end of a burnt stick. These would remain until she cleaned the kitchen, coating the walls with fresh whitewash.

Although his father firmly believed that the boy's drawing was a waste of time, he did little to deter him. In fact, when working by a lamp in the evening, John made room for his son to share the light at the end of his bench. For Christina, the drawings were a source of genuine pride. She enjoyed hearing her husband's customers comment on the images of acrobats and animals that enlivened her kitchen. A family legend records that the unorthodox wall display caught a customer's eye when he came to pick up his shoes, and, upon hearing that young Roberts had drawn them, he asked Christina about the family's plans for their talented son. She responded that eventually he would take his place at the cobbler's bench with his father, but the customer urged the parents to reconsider and allow the boy to train as an artist. To explore their son's future in this line, the parents took a selection of David's drawings to Thomas Graham, a master of the Trustees' Academy in Edinburgh. Although Graham was impressed with Roberts's natural ability, he took into consideration the family's limited income and urged the parents to apprentice him to a house painter. Graham reasoned that, after the boy learned a reliable trade with a dependable income, he could pursue training at the academy with his own means.

In Roberts's youth, the fashion for elaborate interior design transformed house painting from a humble trade into a highly skilled craft. Wealthy clients expected a decorative painter to deliver a wide range of effects, including complex patterning, faux finishes, and spatial illusions. The best practitioners were masters of *trompe l'oeil*, who could deceive the eye by disguising prosaic surfaces with sumptuous brushwork. A flat ceiling could be opened to the sky with a false oculus or given depth with the illusion of carefully hewn masonry vaults. A shallow room could be deepened by the suggestion of niches and arches or could be opened up with a painted window looking out on a scenic garden. The decorative painter gave the effect of rich material on plain surface, emulating exotic woods, aged paneling, and rare marble.

Roberts was barely eleven years old when he entered the workshop of Gavin Beugo, and his apprenticeship lasted seven years. Although little is known of Beugo's style or level of expertise, he had a solid reputation as a decorative painter. As the youngest apprentice in the shop, Roberts was given the most menial tasks: sweeping the floor, grinding the colors, and stirring the vats. His sharpest memory of the shop, which he opened every morning, was its stench—it reeked of hide-glue—and he dubbed it "Botany Bay." Beugo was temperamental and tyrannical, treating the older apprentices with disdain and selecting favorites among the new ones, but he taught Roberts invaluable basics of the trade, including illusion and rapid execution, as well as how to use technical and mechanical processes to simplify the labor.

Working for Beugo left Roberts with little leisure time. He continued to draw on his own, and he organized a small drawing studio with a few like-minded

Plate 1:2 *Departure of the Israelites,* 1829. Oil on canvas, 54 x 72 in. (137.2 x 182.9 cm). Birmingham Museums and Art Gallery.

Plate 1:3 *Gaucin, Looking towards Gibraltar and the Coast of Barbary,* 1834. Sotheby's, London.

apprentices who would take turns modeling for each other. Whenever possible, he returned to the Earthen Mound. Now he could afford the cheapest entry fee to see the theatrical presentations that had tempted him as a little boy. He also became an avid, if eclectic, reader, often spending his lunch money at the "penny library." Scottish culture fascinated him, and he read Hugo Arnot's *History of Edinburgh* and Sir Walter Scott's *Border Ballads.* He also liked tales of adventure; he counted *Blackbeard the Pirate, Gil Blas,* and *Don Quixote* among his favorites. Fortune-telling books appealed to his imagination; from one, which used the location of birthmarks and moles to predict a person's future, he learned that a mark on his leg indicated that he was destined to become a great traveler. Years later he recalled: "This pleased me much, and after the wandering life I have led I have sometimes thought that mole might have had something to do with it."

In 1815, Roberts left Beugo's shop to accept his first independent decorating job in Perth. But when he returned to Edinburgh the following year, he did not find employment. A friend made an unusual suggestion: James Bannister, who ran a ring circus on the Mound, was looking for a scene painter. At first Roberts hesitated, fearing his lack of theatrical experience would make him an unlikely candidate, but the appeal of the challenge—as well as a wage almost double that of house painting—gave him the courage to apply. Bannister hired him, and Roberts later reflected that perhaps he was better suited for the job than he had realized: "For my knowledge was chiefly

derived from the scenery of the Edinburgh Theatre Royal, as seen from the Shilling Gallery."

Bannister's troupe traveled throughout northern England, giving Roberts his first opportunity to see the world beyond the environs of Edinburgh. He enjoyed the peripatetic life and often walked on his own, behind or ahead of the company. They performed in Carlisle, Newcastle, Hull, and York, and, whenever they were booked into a theater, Roberts used the opportunity to study the scenes painted by the resident professionals. On occasion he even performed with the troupe, working with the clowns as a straight man. But his fondest memory of traveling with Bannister's circus was the company's sojourn in York at the end of the season in autumn 1816. He had completed most of the work the performances required, and he used his free time to wander the countryside, making sketches of the local sights. Sitting long hours, often in the rain and snow, he trained his hand and eye in accuracy, observing every detail of the Gothic monuments of York with what he recalled as "a lover's first love and devotion." It was in York that Roberts believed he "first became a painter."

Back in Edinburgh in 1817, Roberts supplemented his sporadic theatrical jobs with house painting. The following year, he secured a position with the Edinburgh Pantheon, working as an assistant to the resident scene painter, Mr. Deerlove. Deerlove also performed with the company, and, exhausted by

Plate 1:4 *The Chapter House, Burgos Cathedral,* 1832. Pencil and wash.
Fine Arts Society, London.

his attempts to rehearse all day and paint all night, he relied heavily on Roberts. One evening, when Roberts noticed that it "pleased God to visit [Deerlove] with a most profound and comfortable snooze," he took the initiative and painted a scheme of his own, an illusionistic view of the Roman Forum, which was intended as the backdrop for the production of *The Silver Swan.* During the opening performance, when Roberts's scene was revealed, an astonished audience recognized that the spectacle before them was far beyond Deerlove's limited ability, and they broke into wild applause.

Roberts's bold display caught the attention of the management of the Theatre Royal in Glasgow, and when the Pantheon closed in 1819, Roberts took advantage of the Royal's offer to have him work in residence. Alexander Naysmith (1758–1840) had preceded him in the position. A meticulous realist, Naysmith left to pursue a career as a landscape painter. Many of his flats were still in use, and Roberts studied them to improve his technique. Roberts's own growing reputation won him an invitation to return to Edinburgh to paint scenes for a production of Scott's *Heart of Midlothian* at the city's Theatre Royal, and in October 1820 he accepted the offer of a resident position there. In Edinburgh he met the aspiring marine painter Clarkson Stanfield (1793–1867), who was working as a scene painter with a London company visiting the city. Sharing interests as well as circumstances, Roberts and Stanfield began a lifelong association of collaboration and friendly competition.

Roberts intended to build a new life in Edinburgh. He had met Margaret McLachlan in 1819 and had married her in Glasgow early the next year. She may have been an actress—she was slim and blonde, three years his junior, and Roberts was smitten by her delicate appearance, claiming he married for "beauty" as well as "pure love." On 4 June 1821, their only child, Christine, was born. Roberts's devotion to his daughter endured throughout his life, but his marriage was brief, for Margaret proved to be a difficult mate, fond of argument and alcohol. The couple often lived apart until Roberts secured a separation from her in 1832.

Like his marriage, Roberts's career did not go as he expected. He was swindled out of payment for an extensive scene-painting job in 1820. He also failed to launch a debut as a landscape painter in 1821, when the oil painting of *New Abbey, Dumfriesshire* (unlocated) was rejected for exhibition by the Fine Arts Institution in Edinburgh. In August 1822, he was dismissed by the Theatre Royal, so he left for London, hoping to change his luck and advance his career.

He found work in London painting sets at the Coburg Theatre, where he renewed his acquaintance with Clarkson Stanfield. Later in the year, Roberts left the Coburg for a position at the more prestigious Drury Lane. Despite his dismissal from the Theatre Royal in Edinburgh, he had left on good terms, and,

until 1830, he returned there each year to provide scenery for the Christmas pantomime. Although his theater designs were much in demand, Roberts hoped to make his name as a landscape painter. In 1824, three of his works—*Dryburgh Abbey, The Front of Melrose Abbey,* and *The South Transept of Melrose Abbey* (all unlocated)—were accepted for exhibition by the Society of British Artists, and two were sold. He was also elected into the society's membership. His subjects were all based on sights from his sketching trips at home in Scotland, and this established his favorite practice: to choose a destination for sightseeing and sketching and to work up his sketches into finished oil and watercolor paintings upon his return to the studio.

Also in 1824, Roberts undertook a shared commission with Stanfield to paint a grand panorama of *The Bombardment of Algiers,* to be toured on the continent. Spectacular visual illusions, such as panoramas (long, painted scenes wound on a drum and rolled out to achieve the effect of a moving image) and dioramas (transparent flats painted and arranged in sequences of two or three to give the illusion of three dimensionality) were in great demand as popular entertainment, both in England and abroad. Exciting subjects, such as battles and disasters, were particularly favored. Roberts and Stanfield worked together on a series of these spectacles: In 1827, they painted four gigantic dioramas in oil (believed to measure nearly thirty by forty feet) for the Queen's Bazaar in Oxford Street, Stanfield handling the marine subjects,

A View of the Lago Maggiore and *The Kent East Indiaman on Fire,* and Roberts painting romantic travel views, *St. George's Castle, Windsor* and *The Ruins of Tintern Abbey.* The exhibition drew record crowds, and Stanfield and Roberts were rehired to paint new scenes for display in 1829. Roberts's subjects were *The Interior of St. Sauveur, Caen* and *The Temple of Apollinopolis, Egypt,* while Stanfield's included *York Minister on Fire,* an ironic selection: before the show could open, the Queen's Bazaar burned to the ground.

Roberts left Drury Lane for Covent Garden in autumn 1826. He immediately took on an extensive project, painting seventeen scenes for a new production of Mozart's *Abduction from the Seraglio* (1782), which he completed without any assistance. When the opera opened on 24 November 1827, the fabulous illusions he had created on stage dazzled the critics. The *New Monthly Magazine* exclaimed, "The scenery is, without exception, the most beautiful we have ever seen in a theatre." Roberts's engagement at Covent Garden kept him working in the theater for the rest of the decade. He provided the scenes for the annual Christmas pantomime. He recreated naval battles, polar expeditions, and the Russian Army marching into Turkey for panoramic displays. In 1829, he painted a new drop curtain, featuring a statue of Shakespeare enshrined in a temple, flanked by Thalia and Melpomene (the muses of comedy and tragedy) with the other muses gathered behind. The *New Times* described the effect as "magical," giving the illusion of "a fourth side of the theatre," tempting the viewer to imagine that "he can walk right through the canvas."

Roberts struggled to gain recognition in landscape painting equal to his achievement in theatrical design. In the spring of 1825, he sent a painting of *The West Front of Notre Dame, Rouen* (private collection) to the Society of British Artists for display at the Suffolk Street Gallery. He had taken a trip to France the previous year and used his travel sketchbook as a rich resource for subjects. The painting was purchased by Sir Felix Booth.

The following year, Roberts made his Royal Academy debut with an exterior view of *Rouen Cathedral* (private collection) that caught J. M. W. Turner's interest, prompting him to comment: "Here is a man we must have our sights upon." The press agreed, and the *Times* noted that Roberts's "pencil seems to acquire force and beauty in every new picture." Roberts also acquired wealthy and admiring patrons, including Lord Northwick, who encouraged him to devote more time to his landscape painting and exhibit only at the Royal Academy. But Roberts felt a sense of loyalty to the Society of British Artists, who had given him his first opportunity to exhibit, and remained active in that institution, serving as vice-president (1830) and president (1831), until his election as an associate member of the Royal Academy in 1838.

Full recognition of his powers as a painter came in 1829 with the exhibition of *Departure of the Israelites* (Plate 1:2) at the Suffolk Street Gallery. It was painted on commission for Lord Northwick, although Roberts chose the subject. With its high point of view, offering a vast scenic overview of the biblical drama, the painting displayed Roberts's full theatrical powers.

The grand and meticulously rendered architecture dominates the composition, making the milling mass of figures almost incidental. The critics trumpeted the work as an extraordinary technical achievement, dwelling on the spectacular aspects of Roberts's composition. The *Morning Journal* claimed that the artist depicted "tens of thousands of the chosen people" and "Egyptian architecture" that was "splendid in the extreme." Many critics compared Roberts's style to that of John Martin (1789–1854), whose apocalyptic visions of biblical tales such as *The Fall of Babylon* (1816) and *Belshazzar's Feast* (1826) excited the same enthusiasm that drew the crowds to panoramic spectacles. Roberts claimed that he had selected his subject for the challenge of painting "that grand although simple style of architecture," rather than for its biblical reference or dramatic potential. But not having seen Egypt or studied in great depth any record of its history, Roberts relied upon his imagination to stage-manage the scene. The astute critic of the *Weekly Review* acknowledged that the theatrical aspect of Roberts's work was not in its dramatic narrative but in its spectacular illusion: "As a piece of pictorial effect—as a specimen of *scene-painting* on a small scale—it is wonderful." The work was shown again to great acclaim in 1830 at the Scottish Academy in Edinburgh, and an engraving of it, published by Moon, Boys, and Company, brought in impressive sales.

In the wake of his new success, Roberts set off in the summer of 1830 on a sketching tour of the Rhine, stopping at Frankfurt, Cologne, Heidelberg, and Mannheim. The sketches he made there allowed him to break into

Plate 1:5 *Interior of the Cathedral at Burgos*, 1835. Oil on panel, 21¾ x 12 in. (55.2 x 30.5 cm). Tate Gallery, London.

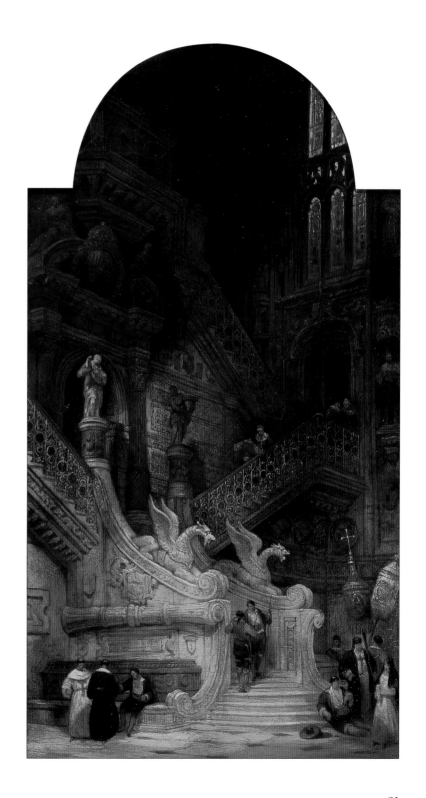

another lucrative art market: selling landscape drawings to publishers to be engraved as book illustrations. Although most of these appeared with texts on travel, culture, and history, the great popularity of landscape views encouraged publishers to feature them in all types of books, including poetry and literature. Twenty-seven steel engravings after Roberts's German sketches were published by Saunders and Otley as illustrations in Edward Bulwer-Lytton's *Pilgrims of the Rhine* (1834). The deep shadows that engulfed Roberts's precise renderings of ancient monuments, looming cliffs, and rugged harbors matched the Gothic gloom of Bulwer-Lytton's melodramatic descriptions. Roberts became one of the most sought-after designers for landscape illustrations, with his credits including *Landscape Illustrations of the Bible* (London: W. and E. Finden, 1836) and several volumes in the series published as *The Landscape Annual* (London: R. Jennings, 1835–1838). Roberts also found regular work "vamping up" the designs of other artists, when their submissions were not up to publishers' standards.

To expand his repertoire and reputation as a travel view artist, Roberts planned a trip to Italy to begin in 1832, but he wrote to D.R. Hay, an old friend from Edinburgh, about choosing another destination. "I think on altering my route from Italy to Spain, as nothing has been done that gives any idea of the magnificent remains of the Moorish architecture which are there." Roberts's change of mind was based on his intense curiosity. While most British artists regarded a trip to Italy as the finishing touch to their education, very few had gone to Spain. Among those who had was David Wilkie (1785–1841), the prominent Scottish genre painter. His journey in 1825 had transformed his work, adding depth, drama, and exoticism to his small-scale, anecdotal style. Wilkie characterized Spain as "wild." Untouched—and therefore unchanged—by tourism, Spain offered a more authentic travel experience than Italy. Roberts was also well aware that Spanish views sketched "on the spot" would be highly marketable because of their novelty. Confident that his journey would be an investment in his career, Roberts used his own savings to finance the trip.

He left England for Spain in October, but his journey was delayed by five weeks due to quarantines imposed on the cities of Bayonne and Irun. He arrived in Madrid in mid-December, and he was surprised by the damp and cold, which he claimed were more bone chilling than a winter in Edinburgh. For the first time in his travels, Roberts felt immersed in an alien culture. While he found the food appalling, writing "I fear I shall never stomach it…. Between oil and garlic it is difficult to tell what you are eating," other unfamiliar aspects of the culture intrigued him. From Madrid, he moved on to Cordoba and then to Granada, where he felt time had stood still since the Middle Ages. He described it to his sister as a place that inspired a "dream of Moors and Christians, tournaments and battles, painting and architecture." The emotional rituals connected with saints' festivals offered a shocking contrast to his strict and plain Protestant upbringing, and he wondered with amusement, "What would my worthy mother think if she saw so many *friskin'* and *loupin,'* like so many antics in the Kirk?"

His wanderlust took him all the way to Gibraltar (Plate 1:3), and then to Morocco, where he had to restrict his movements according to Muslim laws. The cultural differences both shocked and fascinated him; the experience of exotic travel lived up to his boyhood fantasies. He filled many sketchbooks, and he wrote to Hay late in his trip, "It is superfluous to say that my Portfolio is getting rich, the subjects are not only very good but of a very novel character, the only thing is I begin to doubt whether I will ever be able to paint half of them."

Roberts returned to England on 22 October 1833 with more than two hundred sketches (Plate 1:4). He selected the most exotic examples of Moorish architecture to work up as oil paintings for exhibition. As seen in *Interior of the Cathedral at Burgos* (Plate 1:5), Roberts emphasized the opulence and exuberance of unfamiliar forms to convey the sense of difference he felt in the alien setting. He recorded every detail of the richly carved Escalera Dorada (Golden Staircase) in the cathedral's north transept as he had carefully observed it, but the fiery red light spilling from the stained glass window in the upper right of the composition cloaks the meticulous rendering in theatrical drama.

As he had expected, Roberts had no difficulty interesting publishers in his Spanish sketches. Robert Jennings arranged for Roberts to supply enough drawings for four volumes of the *Landscape Annual.* These were published in sequence, featuring different regions of Spain: *Granada* in 1835; *Andalusia* in 1836; *Biscay and the Castiles* in 1837; and *Spain and Morocco* in 1838. Each volume had a text by Thomas Roscoe, who had made his own journey to Spain in 1835. The books were a tremendous success; the first volume sold out its initial run of twelve hundred in two months. Critical acclaim matched popular reception; the *Athenaeum* praised Roberts's "consummate skill," while the *Literary Gazette* reflected that "a more picturesque and romantic series of views is impossible to conceive." Central to nearly every assessment of the work was the fact that Roberts had made the journey himself, rising above artists' common practice of using sketches made by amateur travelers as the sources for their designs. Roberts's contract with Jennings was not exclusive, so he also provided the designs for a series of lithographs made by the publishers Hodgson and Graves for the volume *Picturesque Views in Spain* (1837). The trip to Spain not only fulfilled Roberts's professional ambitions, establishing him in the forefront of landscape view painters, but also gave him the confidence and the means to undertake a more extensive and challenging trip. Roberts set his sights on a journey to Egypt and the Holy Land.

At the time Roberts planned his journey, western Europe viewed the Middle East through a haze of romantic association. The vast region stretching from the coast of North Africa, across the lands of the eastern Mediterranean, to the western shores of the Arabian Sea intrigued the western mind, but this fascination was rooted in the area's rich—and often mythologized—history, rather than its contemporary culture or geopolitical reality. In the European imagination, the Middle East was frozen in time. It had been the site of ancient peoples who had vanished, and only their ruined monuments commemorated them. It bore witness to biblical history as the location of the most venerated sites in the Judeo-Christian religions. Even in the present, the dominant culture, shaped by Islamic beliefs and Arabic traditions, struck Europeans as so different from their own that they regarded the area as strange and backward. But in this difference was an element of exoticism; the East attracted the West because it seemed so alien. The European designation for the Middle East embodied this sense of difference; the whole of the region—despite individual national identities and cultural diversity—was collectively called *the Orient,* a term that, by its very definition, distinguished West from East.

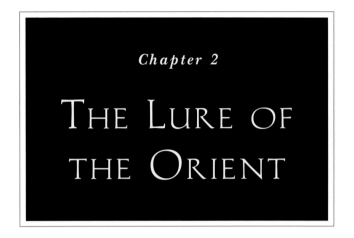

Chapter 2

The Lure of the Orient

The cultural and religious heritage of the Middle East was long characterized by its contrasts with rather than its similarities to Europe. In ancient times, the Western classical cultures of Greece and Rome regarded the nations to the south and east—in Africa and Asia Minor—as barbaric and inferior, of interest only for their trading potential or as targets of political domination. The rise and spread of Islam, beginning in the seventh century and culminating in the eleventh century, heightened the sense of difference felt by the West, and holy wars were mounted to oppose the growth of the new religion. During the thirteenth century, a new political force—the Ottoman Turks—established sovereignty in Asia Minor. For more than three hundred years, the Ottoman Empire expanded, conquering Constantinople in 1483, annexing Egypt and Syria in 1517, and, under the leadership of Sulayman the Magnificent (who reigned 1520–1566), bringing much of the Balkan peninsula and all of Persia under its control. The destruction of the Turkish fleet by European forces at Lepanto in 1571 began the long and steady decline of Ottoman rule; by the early nineteenth century, the once-powerful Turkish Empire was disparagingly known as "the sick man of Europe."

Plate 2:1 Dominique Vivant Denon, *The Great Sphinx at Gizeh,* 1798. From *Travels in Upper and Lower Egypt* (London: T. N. Longman and O. Rees, 1803). Newberry Library, Chicago.

Plate 2:2   *Allegory of the Nile.*
From *Description de L'Egypte*
(Paris: C. L. F. Panckouke,
1809). Newberry Library,
Chicago.

Although Europe shared a history and spiritual roots with the Middle East, the West persistently defined the Orient as its opposite. This is most evident in the enduring symbolic meaning assigned to the region by Western culture: since biblical times, anything or anyone of non-Western origin personified the alien other. In the Old Testament, Solomon's "dark, but comely" bride, Sheba, is a southern—perhaps African—queen. Solomon welcomes her with a loving and passionate song of praise, celebrating her exotic beauty with sensual metaphors of fruits, spices, and scents from distant lands. Similarly, in the New Testament, the Magi who come to pay homage to the infant Christ are described as wise men from the Orient. Their domains are not named, but they have traveled far from their homelands to give the child rare gifts of gold, frankincense, and myrrh. For more than a millennium, this habit endured, and, even though travelers, pilgrims, and Crusaders returned with vivid descriptions of the lands they saw, the image of the Orient as a symbolic realm endured. Depictions of Egypt and the Holy Land were conceived in a farrago of visual fact and fiction; these archaeological absurdities and cultural biases did not disturb the often-well-informed European artist or patron. To the Western mind, the Orient was more a land of fable and mystery than a real destination.

Over the centuries, many intrepid Western travelers did make the arduous journey through the Middle East and recorded their observations. The Greek scholar Herodotus (c. 484–424 B.C.), sometimes called "the Father of History," toured the eastern shores of the Mediterranean during the years 460–455 B.C., visiting many lands, including Babylonia, Scythia, and Egypt.

His impressions appear in his nine-volume *Histories,* ostensibly a secular narrative of the Persian Wars. His narrative is enriched with geographic descriptions of the lands he visited and an eclectic mix of folktales, myths, and anecdotes of customs he observed along the way. For example, after describing the methods used in Arabia to harvest rich spices such as cassia, frankincense, and myrrh, he notes that dangerous adders guard the precious trees, as do "Arabian flying snakes" so vicious that the female devours the male in mating, and the resulting brood devours the mother, even in the womb. In these enthusiastic accounts of natural oddities, set in the respectable context of firsthand observations, Herodotus offers a model of the traveler's tale—part fact, part fascinating fiction—that convinced the audience at home of the existence of worlds of wonder beyond their own borders. Classical writers who followed, including the Greek Strabo (c. 63 B.C.–c. 23 A.D.) and the Romans Diodorus Siculus (fl. first century B.C.) and Pliny the Elder (c. 23–79 A.D.), similarly incorporated in their accounts of history the knowledge gleaned through their personal travels. There is even evidence of tourist activity after the Roman occupation of Egypt in 30 B.C.; some monuments still bear visitors' graffiti in Latin.

When the Roman government adopted Christianity as the state religion under the edict of Constantine (who reigned 310–337), the Bible replaced secular history as the textual repository that gave significance to the world. One of the earliest known Christian travelers was Lady Etheria, a French nun who made a tour of biblical sites in the late fourth century. During her progress through Egypt, she visited the pyramids at Gizeh, then known as Joseph's

Granaries. She inspected hermits' caves and stopped at Thebes. There, she admired the grand Colossi of Memnon, which she tentatively identified as Moses and Aaron, "erected by the Children of Israel in their honor." In subsequent centuries, pilgrims were the dominant travelers to the Holy Land. The rough, and often politically unsettled, conditions of the journey deterred all but the extremely pious, however, and in 637, when Moslems gained control of Jerusalem, most Western travel stopped. From the eleventh century through the thirteenth, under the exhortation of the papacy, Christian nations mounted a series of Crusades in an attempt to take back the sacred city by force (it was briefly captured in 1099 and recovered by Saladin in 1187). The Christian warriors often returned home with more treasures and fabulous tales than renewed faith. Increased trade followed in the wake of the Crusades.

The most extensive—and infamous—traveler's account from the late medieval era remains *The Voiage and Travaile of Sir John Mandeville, Knight*. "Sir John," a knight of the court of Edward III, undertook a pilgrimage to the Holy Land in 1322, but his journey took him much farther than his intended destination, and he passed through most of the kingdoms of the known world. His book, like his identity, is pure fabrication (the author is speculatively identified as Jean d'Outremeuse). But this literary fraud was a popular success; three hundred different manuscripts and more than one hundred printed editions in most major European languages have survived.

Although presented as a guidebook for pilgrims, *The Voiage and Travaile of Sir John Mandeville, Knight* is a compendium of folklore, tall tales, and oddities. Sir John went and was received everywhere: Arabian kings introduced him to their many wives; the king of Java showed him his riches. He saw human marvels, such as wing-eared Scythians and Ethiopian babies born white who miraculously became black at their first exposure to the burning sun. He confirmed that the pyramids were built on the order of Joseph to store the grain needed to endure the lean years prophesied in his dreams. Sir John dismissed other explanations, including the possibility that they were tombs, as "common Rumour." His itinerary in Egypt and the Holy Land included traditional sites of Judeo-Christian significance: the burial grounds of the Patriarchs, the cave where Adam and Eve made their home after the expulsion, and Jerusalem, a city that "hath been in many divers Nations' hands, and often, therefore hath the Country suffered much Tribulation for the Sin of the People that dwell there." Many of Sir John's tales were preposterous; many of his destinations inaccessible. But his text challenged any accusation that it was based on hearsay, for he repeatedly insisted that he had seen it all with his own eyes. His tales intrigued the readers and listeners of Europe; the broad desire of the Western public to believe in the tantalizing strangeness of distant lands gave his outlandish observations credibility.

By the end of the fifteenth century, economics and science had provided additional incentives for travel. The dominant nations of Europe were

Plate 2:3   *Vue des Deux Colosses.* From *Description de L'Egypte* (Paris: C. L. F. Panckouke, 1809). Newberry Library, Chicago.

Plate 2:4   Thomas Hosmer Shepherd, *Egyptian Hall in Picadilly*, 7 June 1828. Engraving, A. McCarthy, engraver; Jones and Company, publisher. Museum of London.

competing for trade routes to the East, mounting voyages of exploration that eventually encircled the globe. In addition to finding new sources for commerce, expeditions documented foreign biology, botany, and culture. Close observation of the natural world informed the new inductive method of science first delineated by Francis Bacon (1561–1626), who asserted that there were two types of knowledge: the one "pure and innocent . . . by which Adam gave name to things" and the other "ambitious and imperious" that tempted Adam and Eve to try to possess moral knowledge, a privilege beyond human grasp. Bacon advocated a healthy curiosity about the observable world as a means to appreciate divine work.

With curiosity transformed from a venial sin into a scientific endeavor, travelers' tales gained legitimacy but were now held to a higher standard. Tangible evidence of exotic wonders helped convince an increasingly skeptical public. For example, when Pietro della Valle (1586–1632) journeyed to Egypt, he returned with vivid descriptions of the site of Gizeh and its surrounding monuments, but he also toted back two mummies to illustrate embalming practices. In Europe, collections of specimens gathered from distant lands—including ancient artifacts, botanical rarities, and biological aberrations—attested to an owner's erudition, but these "cabinets of wonders" were as prized for their strange contents as for what could be learned by studying them. Egyptian mummies were particularly sought after by European collectors. Aside from its value as a macabre souvenir of an alien culture, embalmed flesh was believed to have an unmatched medicinal power. In *Hydriotaphia, or Urn Burial* (1658), Sir Thomas Browne included instructions for the pharmaceutical use of "mumiya" as well as a historical account of embalming practice, claiming "Mummy is become merchandise . . . and Pharaoh is sold for balsam."

In contrast, little evidence of the cultural habits of the contemporary people was recorded; European audiences eagerly accepted tales of fabulous Arabian kings who lived in unimaginable luxury, satisfying lustful and violent appetites with their harems and their tribal wars. The sensuous, exotic life of the Orient described by returning Crusaders endured through the nineteenth century; cultural misunderstanding fed the romantic imagination.

In 1798, Napoleon Bonaparte launched an invasion of Egypt. His strategy was to take advantage of the Ottoman Empire's declining control of the area. The Mamelukes, originally slaves brought into the region by the Fatimid caliphs in the tenth century, had been forced into submission by Turkish forces in 1517, but in the later eighteenth century they had reasserted their power, and, at the time of Napoleon's incursion, their rule was nearly autonomous. Claiming that his mission was to restore control to the Ottoman Empire, Napoleon massed a force of forty thousand troops in Alexandria. But the people of Egypt rallied against him, and the British navy, under the command of Admiral Horatio Nelson, destroyed the French fleet in the Battle of Aboukir Bay. On land, Napoleon's forces brought the Mamelukes into submission in 1799, but their leader Murad Bey eluded the French, so a regiment led by General

Louis Desaix pursued him along the course of the Nile. Once again the British intervened, and, in 1801, they forced the French to withdraw.

Out of this military defeat came a triumph for scholarship. To accompany his forces in Egypt, Napoleon had recruited an army of savants to document the physical and cultural conditions of the region, as the foundation for his planned French colonization of the Nile Valley. The Scientific and Artistic Commission was founded under the direction of Claude-Louis Berthollet, a physician and chemist, and it included a remarkable range of 167 talented experts, with specialties in botany, zoology, paleontology, engineering, and Oriental culture. They brought not only their expertise but also an enormous library, comprising nearly every known volume published on the Nile and its environs, and the scientific instruments they needed to document their findings. The commission was housed in Cairo, in a palace appropriated by Napoleon for the establishment of his Egyptian Institute. Its work lasted three years, and the result was the most accurate and detailed record of European observation of Egypt and its heritage to date.

A contingent of the scholarly commission accompanied Desaix's troops as they tracked Murad Bey up and down the Nile. The scientists made a careful record of the antiquities of the whole region, measuring monuments, recording their state of preservation, and making meticulous renderings of all the notable sites. Among the scholars was Dominique Vivant Denon (1747–1825), formerly the supervisor of the royal collection of antique gems and a diplomat

during the regime of Louis XV. Denon was also a talented draftsman, and he kept a lively journal of the commission's activities. Upon his return to Paris in 1802, he published his impressions of the expedition in *Voyage dans la Basse et la Haute Egypte*. This account presented a vivid and highly personal view of the commission's work, and Denon often stressed the dangers surrounding the scholarly endeavor. He attributed any lapses in his account to the difficulty of the situation, remarking, "Kind reader, please to recollect that we are surrounded with Arabs and Mamelukes, and that, in all probability, I should be made prisoner, pillaged, and very likely killed, if I had thought proper to venture only a hundred paces" away from the protection of Desaix's forces. His enthusiasm for the wonders seen on the expedition enlivened his descriptions. He wrote of the Sphinx at Gizeh: "Though its proportions are colossal, the outline is pure and graceful; the expression of the head is mild, gracious, and tranquil; the character is African; but the mouth, the lips of which are thick, has a softness and delicacy of execution truly admirable; it seems real life and flesh." Many of his drawings portrayed the scholars at work, busily taking their measurements and recording their observations in sketchbooks (Plate 2:1).

Written with wit and verve, Denon's *Voyage* appealed to a wide audience as an adventurous traveler's tale; an English translation appeared in 1803 and was marketed in Britain and America. Denon also scooped the work of the commission. But in 1809, when the commission published its official findings, *Description de L'Egypte*, consisting of twenty-two grandly illustrated folio volumes,

Plate 2:5   John Martin, *The Seventh Plague of Egypt*, 1823. Oil on canvas, 57 x 84 in. (144.8 x 213.3 cm). Museum of Fine Arts, Boston.

this set commanded a singular position as the authoritative study of the land and its history. An allegory of its purpose appeared as the frontispiece to the first volume (Plate 2:2). A telescopic view records the known length of the Nile, with its venerable monuments arrayed along its banks: on the west the view encompasses Gizeh with its Sphinx and a pyramid, the temple at Dendera, the Colossi of Memnon, and the site of Edfu, while on the east are the Obelisk of Heliopolis and the ruins at Karnak, Luxor, and Kom Ombo. Here were all the wonders of Egypt, presented in unprecedented completeness. In addition to meticulous renderings of the monuments of the ancient world, the encyclopedic *Description* documented every physical aspect of the region, including botanical and biological specimens, artifacts and fragments, and a vast array of mummified human and animal remains. The illustrations, reproduced as full-page engravings based on the drawings of the scholars, were composed in a straightforward manner and delineated in a dry, accurate style. But the grandeur and magisterial scale of the subject often gave drama to the rendering, for example in the *Colossi of Memnon at Thebes* (Plate 2:3). With the *Description,* the commission fulfilled its purpose, viewing the region with a scholar's insight and mapping the culture with unmatched scientific precision.

After ousting the French in 1801, the British occupied Egypt for six years under the terms of the Treaty of Alexandria. In its original draft, the treaty required the commission to drop all its claims on artifacts gathered during its expedition and to relinquish its record of the region. The members protested, offering themselves as hostages if their notes were to be held. The final version of the treaty allowed the commission to keep and publish its findings if it forfeited the antiquities on its official inventory. Further protest arose over the most coveted item on that list: the Rosetta Stone, a slab of basalt with inscriptions in hieroglyphics, demotic, and Greek. The British allowed the French scholars to take an ink impression of the face of the stone, but the stone itself was shipped to London. It was housed first in the Library of Antiquaries and later in the British Museum. The scholars' instincts about the significance of the Rosetta Stone proved accurate; in 1822, Jean-François Champollion (1790–1832) used the triple inscription to make the first translation of Egyptian hieroglyphs.

The furor over the Rosetta Stone was only the first incident in a heated contest among European scholars for possession of Egyptian artifacts. For Britain, it was almost an official policy; upon taking the position of consul general in 1816, Henry Salt (1780–1827) was urged by Sir Joseph Banks, a trustee of the British Museum, to use the opportunity to fill the national collection. Salt was happy to comply, and to this end he employed a number of treasure hunters. The most successful—and notorious—was Giovanni Baptista Belzoni (1778–1823), a giant of a man whose checkered career included stints as an actor, an engineer, and a circus strongman. Born in Padua, he had studied hydraulics in Rome and came to Egypt from England in 1815 to work as an engineer for Mehemet Ali, the reigning Turkish governor, or pasha. When

Belzoni's plans for building hydraulic machines failed, Salt hired him to remove a colossal granite figure from its site at Thebes to ship to the British Museum. Belzoni was successful in transporting the sculpture, which he dubbed the "Young Memnon"; he also initiated several archaeological investigations on his own, including excavation of the Temple of Ramses II at Abu Simbel, the opening of the Tomb of Seti I in the Valley of the Kings, and the discovery of the entrance to the Pyramid of Chefren at Gizeh. Belzoni also raided the sites he uncovered, selling some of his finds to finance further expeditions and keeping some for his own collection.

While many of the new wave of British travelers to Egypt sought valuable artifacts, others were inspired by intellectual curiosity. By the 1820s, the traditional "grand tour," an extended journey through the art capitals of Europe, intended to complete a gentleman's education, came to include Middle Eastern sites. A writer in the *Eclectic Review* observed in 1824: "How times have altered since the tour of Europe, the grand tour, was the *ne plus ultra* of gentlemen travelers! No one can now pretend to have seen the world who has not made one of a party of pleasure up the Nile or taken a ride on camel back across the Syrian desert." The ability to keep a record of the journey in words or pictures was important to these travelers, and many, like the young architect Charles Barry (1795–1860), who extended his own tour of Italy and Greece to include Egypt in 1818, came home with thick journals and bulging sketchbooks.

Despite the growing tourist trade and the recent events that had turned the attention of Europe to the east, most tourists preferred to view the region as a vast, open-air museum, avoiding and ignoring contemporary culture whenever possible. One exception was Edward William Lane (1801–1876). He first went to Egypt in 1825, for health reasons. Skilled in the use of the camera lucida—a box fitted with a mirror or prism that reflected an image that could be traced—Lane joined the party of scholar John Gardner Wilkinson in his tour of the Nile. Lane learned the local languages and remained in Egypt until 1828. On his return to London, he gathered his observations of contemporary culture in *The Manners and Customs of Modern Egypt* (1836), a book regarded as the first serious ethnography of the region. He addressed diverse topics, from "The Country and the Climate" to "Domestic Life" and "Industry." Filled with careful accounts of life as he saw it, as well as precise but rather dry illustrations based on drawings he had made with the camera lucida, Lane's book enforced the stereotyped image of the exotic Arab as primitive, sensuous, belligerent, and strange. He observed that the present people of Egypt were "more inactive than they were in earlier times" and that an Egyptian laborer was a poor workman, for he tended to "follow his own opinion in preference to that of his employer." The Egyptians appeared to Lane to typify southern populations, ruled by their appetites; as he saw it, the "indulgence of the libidinous passions, [by] the Egyptians, as well as other natives of hot climates, certainly exceed more northern nations." Although

European observers sought an accurate picture of the ancient world, they preferred to preserve their own fantasies about the modern Orient.

Popular entertainments in London at this time reflected the political and cultural engagements in the Middle East, but real events and scientific discovery seemed to heighten—rather than demystify—the Orient's romantic attraction. Some exhibitions featured special effects; for example, *The Battle of the Nile* (1799), painted by Philippe de Loutherbourg (1740–1812), was presented in a darkened room by firelight to enhance the illusion of a ship exploding at night. The Orient was a favorite subject for panorama and diorama displays. Two views of Constantinople were the main feature in 1801 at the Leicester Square Panorama, the theater owned and operated by Robert Barker, an Edinburgh painter who had patented the form in 1787. Barker promoted his exhibition as educational and provided historical and cultural notes for his viewers. Whenever possible, he hired a painter who had visited the featured region and made drawings "on the spot," but the Middle East was still the domain of soldiers and scholars, and theatrical spectacles boasting Oriental subject matter were more commonly based on secondhand sources: the hasty on-site sketches and the visual descriptions brought back after the Egyptian campaign.

The Egyptian Hall in Picadilly, built in 1812, capitalized on the prevailing interest in the Orient (Plate 2:4). Designed by Peter Frederick Robinson, who cited Denon's sketches as his inspiration and source, the facade featured Egyptian architectural elements and two colossal pseudo-Egyptian statues, purported to be Isis and Osiris, by Sebastian Galhagan. The first director, William Bullock, hoped that the extraordinary appearance of the building would draw the public in to see his museum of curiosities. In 1819, J.B. Papworth redecorated the interior to match the exterior style, and the hall began to feature temporary spectacles. Belzoni agreed to premier his collection of Egyptian artifacts there in 1821, supplemented with a reconstruction of the Tomb of Seti I and models of the Temple of Abu Simbel and a pyramid. Lane later claimed that this display had sparked his desire to travel to Egypt.

Biblical subjects in art were also viewed through the romantic lens of the Orient. In his early career, J.M.W. Turner (1775–1851) painted moody but serene views of venerable castles and cathedrals, but the subject *The Fifth Plague of Egypt* (1800; Indianapolis Museum of Art) inspired him to release his high sense of drama. The real master of the biblical spectacle was John Martin, who favored subjects portraying divine judgment—the Deluge or the destruction of Babylon—and used grand atmospheric effects, dramatic color, panoramic composition, and bolts of lightning as a stage designer would. The power of his compositions earned him wide popularity, whether exhibiting his work in fine art galleries or in spectacle halls. *The Seventh Plague of Egypt* (1823; Plate 2:5) typifies what critics called Martin's "terrible sublime." To set his scene, Martin consulted the works of Herodotus, Strabo, and Diodorus, but his theatrical mastery in evoking the catastrophic hailstorm described in Exodus 9:23, drew more interest than his questionable archaeological reconstructions. Paintings such as Martin's blurred the line between fine art and popular entertainment; little wonder that many of his works appeared in replica at the panorama and diorama halls.

In 1829, when David Roberts first won broad critical acclaim with *Departure of the Israelites* (see Plate 1:2), his work was favorably compared to Martin's. Four years later, in 1833, the Royal Bazaar in Oxford Street featured *The Israelites*, in dioramic form, as its main attraction. By this time, Roberts was no longer working for the spectacle halls, and there is no evidence that he had any involvement with the exhibition. But the replica—four times the size of standard dioramas—reaped praise in the press as "The first illustration of Scriptural History ever painted on so grand a scale" and further enhanced his reputation. Biblical subjects continued to appeal to him. Along with Turner and Stanfield, he contributed drawings of the Holy Land that were published as etchings in *Landscape Illustrations of the Bible* (London: W. and E. Finden, 1836). Like the other artists, Roberts had never seen the region, and he was forced to depend upon the travel sketches of others, such as Frederick Catherwood and Leon de Laborde, as models for his illustrations. Although this was common practice, Roberts felt the lure of the Orient, not just because of its exotic charms but also because he desired to see it for himself. His love of travel and sketching on the spot had led him to journey through Spain. Now, in 1838, he saw that he could be the first artist to bring home a vision of the Orient through his own observations.

As a traveler, ready to embark on the journey of his lifetime, Roberts possessed a unique balance of experience and naïveté. His boyhood rambles and his meanderings with theatrical troupes in his early years had sparked his wanderlust. He had built his career as a painter on excursions to Europe, seeking to study his subjects firsthand and gaining recognition for the accuracy of his observations. By the late 1830s, Roberts was a seasoned traveler, and his recent journey to Spain and Morocco had won him admiration as an adventurous spirit, undaunted by alien customs and exotic culture.

Little in his experience prepared him in any way for his travels through the regions of the Middle East, however. A voracious reader since childhood, Roberts lacked a formal education. He had no training in scientific analysis or archaeological investigation. He may have had some fluency in European languages, but he did not know Arabic. While he was well aware of recent expeditions to the region, his knowledge of both the ancient and the contemporary cultures of the lands he planned to visit was limited. Roberts knew of the monuments that distinguished the region, but he did not possess a scholar's command of their history, and he had only a cursory knowledge of

Chapter 3

NAVIGATING THE NILE

the spiritual beliefs that provided the key to their function and iconography. Compared to the French and British scholars who had preceded him, Roberts was an innocent traveler, but he brought to his journey an open mind, a keen eye, and a genuine enthusiasm to see sights he had only imagined. Experience gave him the confidence to make the trip, but naïveté allowed him a fresh and insightful point of view.

Roberts did not leave a detailed record of how he prepared in the early months of 1838 for his journey. Only references in the journal he kept during the course of his trip suggest the scope of his reading, which included Denon's *Voyage;* familiarity with at least the plate illustrations in the *Description de L'Egypte;* Belzoni's work—perhaps his *Narrative of the Operations and Recent Discoveries within the Pyramids, Temples, Tombs, and Excavations, in Egypt and Nubia* (1820); and the popular guidebook *Travels along the Mediterranean* (1822) by Dr. Robert Richardson. While he looked forward to the adventure of his travels, he also made careful plans to ensure that their results would be profitable. He opened negotiations with the Finden Brothers' publishing house, giving it first right of refusal for a set of illustrated volumes based on drawings made during his journey.

Plate 3:1 *Alexandria.* From *Egypt and Nubia* (London: F. G. Moon, 1846–1849).
Library of Congress, Washington, D.C.

In July, he returned to Edinburgh to spend some time with his parents before departing. Throughout the summer, he saw to the necessary details: arranging for his daughter's education and care during his absence, withdrawing his savings to pay upcoming domestic bills and anticipated travel expenses, and obtaining the letters of introduction he would need to secure travel permits once he arrived in Alexandria. For the latter, Roberts turned to William Penrose Mark, whom he had met in Gibraltar during his travels through Spain. As His Majesty's consul in Gibraltar, Mark had the requisite diplomatic connections to help Roberts, and, as Admiral Nelson's secretary in the navy, he was acquainted with influential members of the British enclave in Alexandria. Mark gave Roberts a letter of introduction to Colonel Campbell of the Foreign Office, who could be relied upon to procure the proper documents quickly and give sound travel advice when Roberts arrived. Mark himself had advice for his friend, writing: "You must indeed have plenty to do before so long a march. Take your talent-box with you, and a fig for everything else."

On 31 August, Roberts departed London for the first stretch of his journey, making his way through France to Marseilles, where he boarded the steamer *Dante* to cross the Mediterranean. Stormy weather made the passage rough, and Roberts was pleased to dock in Civita Vecchia for a half day as the skies cleared. But he regretted that his stay on the Italian shore was so brief, writing later to his daughter, Christine, that he had been "within ten hours journey of the eternal city." The next leg of the trip was serene; in six days the steamer pulled into Malta, where Roberts changed ships. From there, he traveled to the Greek island of Lysa, where he boarded a different steamer to take him to the port city of Alexandria. The crowds on this final ship fascinated Roberts; many of the deck passengers were Turkish pilgrims bound for Mecca. Their costumes and daily prayers struck Roberts as "picturesque," and he later recalled "my sketch-book and I were busily employed."

When Roberts's ship landed in Alexandria on 24 September, he was overwhelmed by the new sights and sensations (Plate 3:1). The bustling city, with its diverse people, its Islamic architecture, and its swaying palm trees, was unparalleled in his experience as a traveler. In his letters home he found the scene impossible to describe, claiming it possessed "a different character from anything I had seen." Used to the fairly homogeneous population of Britain, Roberts gazed in wonder at "Turks in rich dresses; negroes, some nude, with Greeks, Jews, and people of all nations." After making his way through the chaotic crowds of the port, where poor porters struggled with one another to provide services to the European passengers, Roberts checked into his hotel and, without pause, began to prepare for his Nile journey.

Following Mark's suggestion, he called on Colonel Campbell who, in turn, introduced him to Robert Thorburn, the British consul general in Alexandria. Thorburn gave Roberts letters of introduction to the reigning pasha, Mehemet Ali, and introduced him to Louis-Maurice-Adolphe Linant de Bellefonds, a French engineer working for the Egyptian government on

Plate 3:2 *View on the Nile: Ferry to Cairo.* From *Egypt and Nubia* (London: F. G. Moon, 1846–1849). Library of Congress, Washington, D.C.

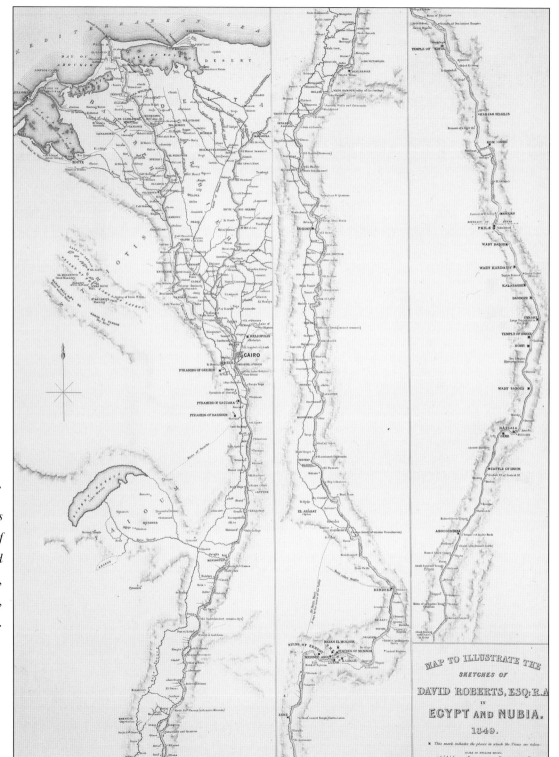

Plate 3:3 *Map to Illustrate the Sketches of David Roberts, Esq: R.A. (1849) of Egypt and Nubia.* From *Egypt and Nubia* (London: F.G. Moon, 1846–1849). Library of Congress, Washington, D.C.

irrigation projects. Twenty years earlier, Linant had accompanied British adventurer William Banks on an expedition to uncover the colossal statues at Abu Simbel. Enthusiastic that Roberts had chosen that site as his most southern destination, Linant offered to escort Roberts around Alexandria to see the "lions," British slang for the major sights. Together they viewed Cleopatra's Needle and Pompey's Column, where Roberts made a few sketches. But Roberts was eager to begin his planned adventure. He concluded his business in Alexandria quickly and, after three days, traveled on to Cairo.

During his brief stay in Cairo, Roberts resided at Hill's Hotel, the only British-owned establishment in the city. As he had in Alexandria, he spent most of his time calling on members of the British foreign service, including the ambassador, and making his final preparations for the journey down the Nile. He rented a boat, a small craft, with a cramped cabin approximately six by five feet and no more than five feet, six inches high. To rid the boat of rats, he had it submerged for a full night in the river, after which it was meticulously scrubbed. At the same time, he engaged the services of an experienced crew of eight men, including a *reis,* or captain, and a local servant named Ismail, who would help him with customs and language. The boat was stocked with a generous store of provisions for three months, as well as bedding for Roberts's cabin, an awning for a portion of the deck, and a Union Jack to fly from the mast (Plate 3:2).

Preparations filled most of Roberts's time, but he made a brief tour of the major sights, as he had in Alexandria. Impressed by the architecture of Cairo's mosques, he decided to delay sketching them until his return. On 3 October, he hired a donkey and a *dragoman,* or guide, and rode to the site at Gizeh. His first glimpse of the pyramids disappointed him; they seemed smaller and less spectacular than he had expected. But, in his attempt to climb the "great one," the Pyramid of Cheops, he acknowledged that the scale was "no joke." The Sphinx, however, enthralled him, and he mused "What sensations run through us at first sight of these stupendous monuments of antiquity."

Roberts set sail on 6 October. It was common practice when traveling the length of the Nile to make the outward journey against the river's flow as rapidly as possible, returning downstream with the current at leisure. This suited Roberts; the journey upstream would afford him an initial look at the monuments (Plate 3:3). The party would stop only at major sites, allowing the crew to rest and restock while Roberts took notes and preliminary measurements. On the return trip, Roberts would make the elaborate on-site sketches that he could use as source material for his studio oils and illustration designs when he was back in London. The interval of time would also allow Roberts to become accustomed to the conditions of light, climate, and atmosphere, so different from any in his previous experience. He knew that his first glimpse of the ancient ruins would stun him; his meticulous method of working required absolute concentration and a steady hand.

Several new acquaintances joined Roberts for the outbound journey. While in Alexandria, he met Captain Nelly of the 99th East Middlesex Regiment, who offered to act as his companion and interpreter. Following in a boat behind was a man named Vanderhost, who traveled with a Maltese servant and an Italian chef, and another man identified by Roberts as "Mr. A.," who joined them in Cairo. In a letter to his daughter, Christine, written at the conclusion of his journey, Roberts admitted that he openly enjoyed the luxurious treatment his status as a Western traveler afforded him. "There I sat, sketch-book in hand, smoking my long Turkish chabouk, with a servant to attend to all my wants, and a boat with eight men at my command to stop or go on as I liked." He claimed to feel "as independent as any king in Christendom."

A seasoned traveler, Roberts expected some discomfort, but he was surprised at the relentless onslaught of insects that plagued his nights on the river. He quickly learned to cover his whole body with a gauze net, and he fashioned gloves to protect his hands while he was sleeping. Despite the precautions he had taken before departure, there were rats on board, and he rationalized that these were of a different kind, water—as opposed to land—rats. Progress was slow in the first few days due to low wind. Although Roberts wrote to his daughter that he was "anxious to get to the extremity" of his outward journey, his diary entries reveal how he steeped himself in the atmosphere. On

15 October, docked for the night at Antaeopolis, he wrote: "The sun was setting, and beaming full upon the hills—deep broad shadows on one side of the amphitheatre, a red purple glow on the other—long lines of green maize here and there broken by the palm and acacia—the solitary ibis stalking lazily along the banks; altogether the scene was imbued with a serenity and beauty I have never seen equalled."

The winds picked up, and, on 18 October, Roberts and his party reached the midpoint of their outward journey. Dendera was the first major site on Roberts's planned itinerary, and its scale and beauty more than met his expectations. He wrote in his diary that he was "struck with amazement." A two-day stop allowed him to inspect the well-preserved monuments, making a ground plan of the site and a cursory elevation drawing of the temple's facade. The number and variety of figures that graced the temple—massive heads sculpted on columns, reliefs incised into the walls, bands of figurative painting—intrigued Roberts, and he noted that they ranged from gigantic forms, more than fifteen feet high, to "others so small they require to be examined by a glass." The meaning of the figures, and the hieroglyphs that accompanied them, hardly concerned him. Roberts intended to capture the view and evoke the visual sensation, leaving analysis to historians and archaeologists.

After Dendera, on 23 October, Roberts entered the Valley of the Kings (Plate 3:4). At Luxor, he hired a local guide to assist him in climbing the Propylon and taking measurements. Reading Denon's *Voyage* had raised his expectations

Plate 3:4 *General View of the Ruins of Luxor from the Nile.* From *Egypt and Nubia* (London: F. G. Moon, 1846–1849). Library of Congress, Washington, D.C.

Plate 3:5 *Wady Dabod, Nubia (Wadi Dabod).* From *Egypt and Nubia* (London: F. G. Moon, 1846–1849). Library of Congress, Washington, D.C.

about the massive scale of the ruins of Thebes, and he was not disappointed. At Karnak, the pillars, more than thirty-three feet in circumference, made "a man beside them look a pigmy." But seeing the monuments set upon the vast plain made him doubt Denon's account. The savant had claimed that, when the French army caught its first sight of the "gigantic phantoms," the men had "suddenly and with one accord, stood in amazement at the sight of the shattered ruins, and clapped their hands with delight." Roberts later told William Brockedon, author of the text for his volumes on Egypt and Nubia, that the incident was likely Denon's fabrication. "It is only on coming near that you are overwhelmed as it were with astonishment; you must be under them and walk around them and for this reason I am fearful painting will scarcely convey any notion of what I mean."

Throughout the outbound journey, Roberts took advantage of weather delays and random stops for supplies to leave the boat to explore the villages and mingle with the people who lived near the shore. Captain Nelly often went with him, and one morning they were approached by two shy, beautiful young women, who shared with them a basket of dates and freshly baked brown bread. The encounter typified the generous and spontaneous hospitality that Roberts came to understand as customary, and he regretted that he had "not even Arabic . . . to thank them." At Thebes, the party was entertained by a troupe of six dancing girls. In describing them, as in many of his remarks, Roberts noted the racial mix among the women, commenting that only three of the six were in fact good dancers, and the best of those was

"a black girl, elegant in person and equally graceful in her dancing with one of the most expressive countenances I ever beheld." As for the men he encountered, Roberts noted a striking difference between ethnic Egyptians and Turks, observing that the latter were always "armed to the teeth."

He seemed less interested in the natural life of the region, except when it came to crocodiles. He regarded them with a horrified fascination, and his diary records anecdotes about their gruesome feeding habits as well as the times he sighted them. The first occasion was 18 October near Dendera, where at least half a dozen of the giant reptiles—some fourteen feet in length—were sunning themselves on a sandbank. Roberts and his crew shouted to clear them away, and he was amazed that, despite the racket, the crocodiles were unmoved by human presence. Later in his journey he made sketches of a small group on the shore at Wadi Dabod, where he had seen a giant of the species, at least twenty feet long (Plate 3:5). With them, he depicted a small flock of herons, said to feed off the parasites that lived on the crocodiles' scaly hides. Although fascinated by the gory details in accounts of these monsters devouring men and beasts from nearby villages, Roberts and the members of his party refrained from shooting a crocodile for a trophy—although this had become the prized emblem of the adventurous Nile traveler.

Roberts and his crew picked up their pace again after their brief visit to the Valley of the Kings. Within a week they had passed Esna, Edfu, and Kom Ombo, to arrive at the First Cataract at the end of October. At this point on the Nile, where the river branches, peaks of granite rock and several islands slowed their progress. At the head of these obstructions was the island of Philae, which Roberts described as "a paradise in the midst of desolation." Locally known as Giesirel el Berbe el Ghassir (Island of Ruined Temples), this small island, not more than fifty acres, was the site of four temples, including one consecrated to the great triad of Egyptian deities, Osiris, Isis, and Horus. Roberts chose to delay his passage through the rapids of the First Cataract to draw the Hypaethral Temple, commonly known as "Pharaoh's Bed," based on the belief, now discredited, that the sovereign resided there when visiting the island (Plate 3:6). It was, in fact, built by Trajan to house the sacred boat of Isis in 105 A.D., and the designation *hypaethral* denotes the absence of a roof. Although aware of both names, Roberts believed the structure to be at least two thousand years old, remarking that "the details of the decorations are so clear as to suggest that the stone cutters have only finished work."

On 1 November, the two boats crossed the First Cataract. It took another week to reach their final destination, the site of Abu Simbel, located 530 miles south of Cairo. They docked at night, and on the morning of 9 November Roberts eagerly disembarked to see the monument that he claimed made the arduous journey to Nubia worthwhile. The most striking feature of the gigantic rock-cut temple, built by Rameses II (who reigned 1290–1224 B.C.), was its four colossal enthroned figures of the Pharaoh, each over sixty-five feet high (Plate 3:7). Roberts explored the site, including the temple interior, which had been opened by Belzoni in 1817. Spending three days at Abu Simbel, Roberts made at least four detailed studies of both the interior and the facade. He lamented that the site had become popular with "Cockney tourists and Yankee travellers," who often chipped fragments and left their mark in the form of graffiti. He found it "appalling" to see the dignified colossi "covered with the signatures of every Tompkins, Smith, and Hopkins . . . who, not content with having taken a finger of the great statue as a souvenir of their deplorable exploit, have then had the gall to carve their stupid names on the very foreheads of the gods."

While Roberts worked at the site of Abu Simbel, his companions continued on to Wadi Halfa to catch sight of the treacherous rapids of the Second Cataract. Roberts, it seems, had no interest in following them. On 11 November, he parted company with his European companions and turned his own craft around. In his journal, he wrote "At nightfall we began to descend the stream. . . . Thank God our vessel's prow now faces north and civilization." Rather than seek adventures to test his nerve and prowess, Robert sought picturesque subjects to challenge his eye and hand. He now knew what potential Nile views lay before him, and he was eager to transform the sights he had seen into pictures, making the ink-and-pencil sketches and watercolor renderings that would serve as his memory aids in the studio.

Following the conventions of navigating the Nile, Roberts's party traveled downstream at a more leisurely pace. The current now carried them, lightening the boatmen's work. But Roberts's work began in earnest. The outward

Plate 3:6   *The Hypaethral Temple at Philae, Called the Bed of the Pharaoh.* From *Egypt and Nubia* (London: F. G. Moon, 1846–1849). Library of Congress, Washington, D.C.

Plate 3:7   *The Great Temple of Aboo Simble (Abu Simbel)*. From *Egypt and Nubia* (London: F. G. Moon, 1846–1849). Library of Congress, Washington, D.C.

Plate 3:8   *A Group of Nubians, Wady Kardassy (Wadi Kardassy)*. From *Egypt and Nubia* (London: F. G. Moon, 1846–1849). Library of Congress, Washington, D.C.

journey had given him the opportunity to select what he wanted to draw, and his initial investigations allowed him to estimate the amount of time to devote to each site. He expected to carry out his program efficiently. He had also used the outbound journey to get a sense of atmosphere, to acclimate his eye to the region's geography and light, and to experience the sense of awe and wonder stirred by ancient monuments that had long tantalized his imagination. On second sight, he intended to observe and render his studies with customary accuracy. He would recall the power of his first, more romantic responses when he returned to his studio to produce designs for the illustrations he intended to publish.

On 12 November, Roberts arrived in Derr, the capital of Nubia, where he admired the solid and well-tended houses, "cleaner than any in Lower Egypt." But it was the people, rather than the architecture, of the cities of Nubia that Roberts found most memorable. He recorded in his diary that the men were unusually "well-made and handsome, their countenance open and intelligent and their teeth like ivory." He sketched a group of men at Wadi Kardassy, depicting them in their comfortable garments of loose trousers gathered at the waist and ankles, with a mantle of the same cotton tossed over one shoulder (Plate 3:8). Roberts found their hairstyle intriguing, and it reminded him of the headdresses he had seen on the figures of ancient monuments. The men had a short fringe cut across the forehead, a topknot of hair on the crown, and jaw-length plaits. The women were similarly good-looking, but Roberts was repulsed by their practice of coating their skin and

hair with a buttery pomade made from the crushed beans of the castor oil plant. Intended to soften the skin and protect it from sun and insect bites, it gave off a rancid odor that, for Roberts, detracted from their beauty.

From Derr he traveled to Korti, where he sketched a group of Nubian women, the married women in flowing, cotton dresses and the adolescents and children in brief fringed skirts. Unlike the men, the women were disinclined to pose for him, and it troubled him that they often seized their children and ran away at his approach. He soon learned that slave traders were active in Korti, and the women feared any man they did not recognize, particularly if he was white. In his diaries and letters home, Roberts frequently expressed his disgust at the perpetuation of the slave trade, which his own country had banned in 1807. He saw evidence of the appalling practice throughout his journey, and, while in Korti, he sketched a group of Abyssinian women gathered in the shade of a spindly palm tree, under the watchful eye of their Turkish captor (Plate 3:9). Roberts was told that they were bound for the market in Cairo, where young Abyssinian women would bring a high price when sold as harem concubines. Later on the trip, Roberts's boat was approached by a slave ship run by a Greek trader. Roberts noted that there were only eleven women on board, all young and beautiful, bound for a market in West Africa. Seeing them huddled under a thin, dirty sheet in the cold night air angered him. In his diary, he condemned the trader as a "villain" and lamented that he had "too few words of Arabic or Greek to tell the old rascal how much his occupation was abhorred in England."

Abyssinian Slaves resting at Korti — Nubia.

Plate 3:9 *Abyssinian Slaves resting at Korti—Nubia.* From *Egypt and Nubia* (London: F. G. Moon, 1846–1849). Library of Congress, Washington, D.C.

Plate 3:10 *Grand Portico of the Temple of Philae—Nubia.* From *Egypt and Nubia* (London: F. G. Moon, 1846 –1849). Library of Congress, Washington, D.C.

Plate 3:11 *Island of Philae on the Nile.* From *Egypt and Nubia* (London: F. G. Moon, 1846–1849). Library of Congress, Washington, D.C.

Roberts's passage through the cities of Nubia provided a relaxing prelude to his program of work as he descended the Nile. On 16 November, in Wadi Kardassy, he bought a few souvenirs from local merchants, including some copper coins from a woman, and a few small swords, a hippopotamus-hide shield, and a water bottle covered with shells, from a man who also sold him a bracelet right off his arm. Roberts's party then returned to Philae, where he worked for three days, making sketches of the general view of the island and its individual temples. He was particularly intrigued by the Temple of Isis, sketching it from various angles, including a distant view of the court and colonnade, several interior views of the hypostyle hall, and the grand portico at the hall's entrance (Plate 3:10). He made careful note of the rich, brilliant colors that embellished the column capitals, ceiling coves, portal entablatures, and interior ceilings—emerald green, lapis blue, and carnelian red—which have, since Roberts's time, been obliterated by water damage. He also rendered the island's subtle atmospheric effects, which led him later to depict a romantic evocation of Philae at sunset (Plate 3:11).

Plate 3:12 *The Island of Philae—Nubia*. Sotheby's, London.

His next stop was Kom Ombo, where he worked for two days (Plate 3:13); by twilight of 22 November, his party had reached Edfu, where again the effect of the setting sun struck him as picturesque. He worked through the next day at the site, drawing the pronaos of the temple, half buried in the sand. The heat, which had been steadily rising since the beginning of the month, was beginning to interfere with his work. At Edfu, with the temperature nearly 100 degrees, he took cover under a sunshade to sketch but admitted "I did not make a very good job of it." The party picked up speed and by 25 November reached Esna, where Roberts was approached by a group of Coptic Christians, who welcomed him as one of their own, which both amused and confused him.

By 26 November, he was back in Karnak, where he worked for four full days, from dawn to twilight. The colossal ruins provided a spectacular subject for Roberts, and he sketched them from every possible angle: near and afar, above and below. To convey the gigantic scale, he included tiny figures in colorful Turkish garments. Just as he admired the freshness of the architecture at Philae, the ruined state of Karnak's temples sparked his romantic sensibility. He depicted the colonnade of the Great Hypostyle Room in the temple from a high point of view, which emphasized the colossal scale even further and allowed him to portray the mounds of windswept sand around the base of the columns and the precariously tilted column and lintel at the end of the aisle (Plate 3:14). On 29 November, his last working day at the site, he sketched a panoramic view at dawn, the buildings still wrapped in purple shadow, while the foreground figures, composed from his observations of the local populace, are illuminated in the gentle morning light (Plate 3:15). Roberts devoted only one day, 1 December, to Luxor. On his outward journey, he had made a series of preliminary sketches, which he felt would serve to fill in any details that he missed on his return. He drew the monuments dedicated to Rameses II—including the obelisk and the buried colossi—views of the courtyard of the Temple of Amenhotep III, and a panoramic view of the west bank of the Nile as seen from the site. At Luxor, as at Karnak, he selected a high point of view to provide a dramatic vista of the Great Temple of Amun (Plate 3:16). The sanctuary was cluttered with debris and shacks, but Roberts cleared some of them away in his image, positioning a caravan at rest at the entrance. While he often composed his views like stage sets, adding or removing details to enhance an image, he carefully copied two features of this particular site: the hundreds of earthenware pots placed on the roofs of the intruding buildings to serve as dovecotes and the falcon that perched on the tip of the temple's obelisk during the time he was sketching.

It was Roberts's habit to abstain from work on Sundays in observance of his Sabbath, but he rarely used those days for relaxation. While at Thebes, he filled his hours of leisure visiting the nearby village of Qurnah. Mixing with the people as much as his limited knowledge of their languages and customs allowed, he took careful account of costume, gesture, and incident, which he later reconfigured as "local color" in his designs. Sketches of a ruined temple, which he identified as the Temple of Amun at Goorna (a mortuary temple, now attributed to the reign of Seti I), gave him a picturesque setting for

Plate 3:13   *Kom Ombo*. From *Egypt and Nubia* (London: F. G. Moon, 1846–1849). Library of Congress, Washington, D.C.

Plate 3:14 *Karnak*. From *Egypt and Nubia* (London: F. G. Moon, 1846–1849). Library of Congress, Washington, D.C.

Plate 3:15   *Ruins of Karnak.* From *Egypt and Nubia* (London: F. G. Moon, 1846–1849). Library of Congress, Washington, D.C.

Plate 3:16   *Grand Entrance to the Temple of Luxor.* From *Egypt and Nubia* (London: F. G. Moon, 1846–1849). Library of Congress, Washington, D.C.

such a vignette (Plate 3:17). A group of men gather around a water pipe. The central figure—dignified and handsomely dressed—is an agent of Pasha Mehemet Ali. While in Qurnah, the agent collects taxes and settles any disputes over property and legal issues. The sheik of the village stands at the agent's right shoulder, listening intently. At the far left, Roberts placed a woman wearing a *boorcho,* or face veil, gracefully balancing an earthenware jug on her head. Two small boys—in garments that indicate different class status—stand near her. Roberts may have seen a meeting between an agent and the men of the village, but the studied variety of figures, costumes, and actions in the work reveals that he often constructed a visual pastiche for a picturesque effect.

On 3 December, Roberts traveled north through the Valley of the Kings, and spent the whole of the following day making sketches of the Colossi of Memnon in the plain of Thebes. These huge statues of Amenhotep III had been regarded as essential sights to see since the days of the earliest travelers. Christian pilgrims such as Lady Etheria associated them with Aaron and Moses, but the Roman tradition that identified them with the Homeric hero Memnon, slain by Achilles, was far more persistent and gave the site its enduring name. From the Ptolemaic era, travelers had claimed that the northernmost statue emitted a plaintive wail as the sun rose. Although Strabo, in his history, attributed the sound to the trickery of local priests, popular tradition held that each morning Memnon's mother, Aurora, caressed him, and he responded with a sorrowful moan. Greek and Latin inscriptions attest that visitors witnessed the phenomenon, but Roberts and his party heard nothing, for it ceased when the Roman Emperor Septimius Severus (who reigned 193–211) had the upper portion of the colossus restored. It had been damaged in an earthquake in 27 B.C., and the likely source of the wail was the channel of stone where the wind blew through the cracks of the statue.

In his finished illustration designs, Roberts emphasized the grandeur of these magnificent statues, choosing a very low point of view to dramatize the way they dominated the surrounding plain (Plate 3:18). While sketching, he encouraged his crew to scale the lower reaches of the "wailing" colossus, to portray how its size dwarfed humanity. Later, in the studio, Roberts would concoct a spectacular image of the colossi seen from behind in the light of a rose-tinted dawn during the inundation of the Nile (Plate 3:19). The annual rising of the waters began in May or June and crested in October, so Roberts might have been inspired by the river's height on his outbound journey; by December, when he was working at the site, the waters had abated. And perhaps the evocative tint of the image in its final printed form was a tribute to Aurora and her son.

Roberts's next destination was Dendera. His earlier visit had left him with a sense of "amazement" at the variety of decoration and color, as well as the condition, of the facade of Temple of Hathor. He had declared the state of preservation perfect, "except where it had been purposefully defaced." The damage has been associated with Coptic Christianity. Pious monks who

Plate 3:17 *Entrance of the Temple of Amun at Thebes.* From *Egypt and Nubia* (London: F. G. Moon, 1846–1849). Library of Congress, Washington, D.C.

Plate 3:18   *Thebes (The Colossi of Memnon Seen from the Southwest).* From *Egypt and Nubia* (London: F. G. Moon, 1846–1849). Library of Congress, Washington, D.C.

appropriated the temple for their own use had obliterated the face of Hathor—goddess of love and pleasure—from the column capitals. Roberts arrived at the site on 6 December and worked for three days. He spent most of 7 December locating the right point of view to provide a wide-angle vista of the temple facade, capturing both its grand spatial effect and the fine details of decoration (Plate 3:20). He wrote in his diary: "All day at Dendera. After much trouble, got an excellent view of the temple looking inwards. This and an interior were all I could do."

On 9 December, Roberts concluded his work at Dendera and recorded that these sketches completed his planned series of sites along the Nile. "I may not have done them justice," he wrote, "but few artists of my standing could have produced more in the same number of days." He was now eager to return to Cairo, to sort his drawings and to start the second phase of his sketching program: the mosques and citadels of the city. He hoped to rest a bit on the last leg of the return trip, and, on 11 December, his party stopped at Girgeh, where he climbed a mountain and explored nearby caves. Two days later in Siout, he discovered to his tremendous distress that the sketchbook containing his drawings from Nubia was missing. He remembered having it at Girgeh. Rather than have his whole party retrace the eighty miles, Roberts sent his servant, Ismail, and one of his boatmen, Hassan, back to the site on an English ship that was ready to depart. For four days, Roberts waited nervously, trying to distract himself, arranging, fixing, and retouching the drawings he still had with him. He knew that the loss of this sketchbook, which documented the farthest reach of his journey, would drastically reduce the power and selling potential of the project he planned to publish. On 17 December, when the men returned with the lost drawings, Roberts could scarcely express his relief. "The finding of my book was almost a miracle. It was not in the place I had imagined and described to my men, who after ascending the mountain, returned to the cave which I had first entered, where they found the treasure they had come to seek." Once again, the party headed north and on 21 December arrived safely in Cairo.

Upon his return, Robert was greeted with a long, affectionate letter from his daughter, Christine. The news she shared pleased him: she was well, his parents were in good health, and, in his absence, he had been elected an associate member of the Royal Academy of Art in London. He now took a brief but well-earned rest, writing letters home and sorting through the notes and drawings that recorded the wonders of his expedition. In his diary, he summed up the trip as "fascinating, and undoubtedly the most important of my entire life." In a New Year's letter to his friend Hay, he boasted of the breadth of his accomplishment—over a hundred drawings that "approached nearer the thing than any hithertoo"—and added, "Not bad for a month's work."

Plate 3:19 *Statues of Memnon at Thebes during the Inundation.* From *Egypt and Nubia* (London: F.G. Moon, 1846–1849). Library of Congress, Washington, D.C.

Plate 3:20 *Dendera*. From *Egypt and Nubia* (London: F. G. Moon, 1846–1849). Library of Congress, Washington, D.C.

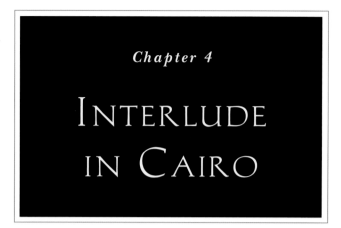

Chapter 4

INTERLUDE IN CAIRO

ROBERTS SCHEDULED A BRIEF INTERVAL in Cairo to rest from the rigors of his recent journey and to prepare for his next expedition. Although he was uncertain how long he would stay, he rented a house, finding it far more economical than returning to Hill's Hotel. On 22 December, one day after docking in Cairo, he moved into his new residence.

Roberts devoted little time to relaxation. Instead, he sorted, reviewed, and retouched the drawings and watercolors he had made on the Nile and caught up on correspondence with family and friends in Britain, sending enthusiastic descriptions of his experiences and of the wonders he had captured in his portfolio. He had to make complex preparations for his trip through Palestine and Syria, purchasing equipment, hiring men and a guide to accompany him, and arranging for camels to carry their provisions. But the most pressing need was paperwork, for Roberts would pass through the jurisdictions of several regional governments, each requiring a travel permit—known as a *firman*—that was authorized by the pasha.

Roberts also wanted to use his time in Cairo to make sketches of the city. With his practiced eye, he recognized the potential for evocative subjects in Cairo's buildings, ranging from venerable ruins to newly built shacks. Rising above all the city's structures were the striking mosques, crowned by domes and minarets. To Roberts, the city looked like a fabulous stage set, confirming all his romantic expectations of the exoticism of the East. But he also recognized that views of contemporary Cairo would give his portfolio a rare distinction. On his last night on the Nile, he wrote in his journal, "Now for Cairo and the architecture of the Moslems, which is not so well known."

Following his favored method, Roberts spent several days wandering around the city to absorb the atmosphere and select subjects to sketch. On 23 December, he visited the Tombs of the Caliphs. The next day he went to the Citadel, the residence of Mehemet Ali, where he was permitted to enter a few rooms in the private apartments. He dismissed them as "all modern, and gaudily painted." Similarly, on 25 December, after seeing the Tombs of the Mamelukes, a new mausoleum commissioned by the pasha, he reflected that the style and construction were crude compared to those of ancient structures. In this, Roberts echoed the common Western view that Islamic rule had caused the decline of Egyptian civilization. In a letter to his daughter on

Plate 4:1   *Mosque El-Mooristan, Cairo.* From *Egypt and Nubia*
(London: F. G. Moon, 1846–1849). Library of Congress, Washington, D.C.

Plate 4:2 Robert Scott Lauder, *Portrait of David Roberts in Turkish Clothing*, 1840. Oil on canvas. Scottish National Portrait Gallery, Edinburgh.

22 December, he attributed the crumbling condition of cities he had seen along the Nile to "misgovernment, and the barbarism of the Moslem creed." Roberts had come to the region with this prejudiced view. British writers such as John Gardner Wilkinson and Edward William Lane, in their respected ethnographies, defined indolence and sensuality as characteristics of the contemporary people of the region. Knowing little of the culture he was about to explore and record, Roberts approached his forays into the city with a biased trepidation, wondering if his endeavor would be met with encouraging curiosity or daunting hostility.

Roberts viewed Cairo with a Western eye, seeing the narrow streets, the splendid mosques, and the throngs of people going about their daily business as undeniably picturesque. It was a crowded city—with more than thirty thousand inhabitants, its population was significantly greater than that of Edinburgh—and its streets were dense with activity. On 26 December, Roberts began to document the major monuments of Islamic architecture, including the Mosque of Sultan Hassan, the Tombs of the Caliphs, and the Tombs of the Mamelukes, but his attention was constantly diverted to Cairo's vital street life, where he endured the stares of the curious and the press of the crowds to make his sketches. For example, the narrow passage leading up to the Mosque of Sultan Qalawun (which he identified as the Mosque El-Mooristan) was lined with shallow shops, and the traffic of merchants carrying goods to and from them, as well as the strolling shoppers, made the street nearly impassable (Plate 4:1). The diversity of the population that swarmed around Roberts amazed him: "Such a scene! All the Eastern nations gathered together. Turks and Greeks in their picturesque costumes. The wild Arab, who never slept within walls, every tribe in different dress and all armed."

Roberts had also never seen such a variety of goods. In his letters to Christine, he admired the way the shopkeepers presided over their wares with dignity and gravity. For the most part, the shops were small, in shallow stalls set into the buildings at the ground level or in temporary tents on the street. The shopkeeper would sit on a platform in front of his establishment, smoking while he waited for a customer. Roberts noted that business was conducted with ceremony, generally over a shared pipe. Most bazaars featured a specific type of goods. The coppersmiths gathered in one district, the cloth merchants in another. Roberts sketched the Silk Mercers' Bazaar, located near the religious complex of Sultan al-Ghuri, a venerable structure from the Fatimid period, founded by Vizier Jawhar al-Siqilli in the last quarter of the tenth century. But the looming presence of the old buildings, and even the staggering array of superb textiles—including silks, fine cottons, and embroidered cloths with gold and silver threads—faded into the background when Roberts depicted the vendors absorbed in negotiations or puffing their pipes as they waited for customers.

His days in the streets of Cairo were not without difficulty. Roberts provided a spectacle for the curious; a British man in Western dress, seated on the street and surrounded by paints, chalks, and brushes, was as odd to the residents of Cairo as they were to him. He took the stares in stride, but he never adjusted to the dense crowds he encountered: "These narrow, crowded streets render it very difficult to make drawings, for in addition to the curiosity of the Arabs, you run a risk of being squeezed to a mummy by the loaded camels, who although they are picturesque in appearance, are ugly customers to jostle." In a New Year's letter to his daughter, he pondered, "No one looking over my sketches will ever think of the trouble the collection of them has cost me."

Roberts experienced only one incident of open hostility. While he was sketching in the Bazaar of the Khan Khalael, which he described as "the Cheapside of Cairo," someone in a building above the bazaar pitched a half-eaten orange at him and knocked his sketchbook from his hand. Roberts never saw his assailant. Realizing that no damage had been done, he put the attack in perspective: "A Turk sketching in Cheapside might not have escaped more easily from interruption, though not in the same way." The days Roberts spent in the crowded streets of the Egyptian capital tempered his prejudiced views. He admired the overall demeanor of the local people, conducting themselves with restraint and civility in uncomfortable circumstances. He balanced the crowded bazaars with tranquil scenes of men relaxing in coffeehouses, and he depicted the individual services offered alongside the goods, as seen in vignettes such as a veiled woman dictating a letter to a scribe. Roberts's experience may not have given him any deep insight into contemporary Islamic culture, but he developed a sympathy for the people, based on his observations of their public dignity and purposeful actions, qualities that ennobled the figures in his final designs for publication.

As he made the rounds of Cairo's streets, Roberts was repeatedly frustrated in his desire to enter the mosques he wanted to sketch. Well aware that Islamic practice excluded men of other faiths from these sacred precincts, Roberts contacted Colonel Campbell to see if there was any means through which he could gain entry. Although Campbell managed to provide Roberts with the papers that allowed him to move freely through the city—as well as a guard who acted as a guide during his tour—he was unable to circumvent the prohibition. On 2 January, Roberts met with Mr. Wane, the vice-consul, who offered a novel solution: that Roberts should adopt the local manner of dress and pass himself off as a Turk.

Roberts was uncomfortable with the suggestion. He did not like having to disguise his identity, and he feared being found out. But, realizing that this was the only way to gain entry, he purchased a caftan, loose trousers, and a cloak of multicolored cotton. He bound his waist with a thick sash and suspended a sword from his belt. A turban covered his hair, but he had to shave his long, fashionable sideburns, for they would have betrayed him instantly as Western. He even discarded his hog's-hair brushes, making certain that he would not enter sanctified spaces with any item that Islamic law regarded as impure. When fully in costume, Roberts was surprised at his own transformation. With his skin well tanned from his recent journey and his dark brown eyes, he made a dashing—and fully credible—appearance as a high-ranking army officer, and he later commented that in full Arabic dress he was "so completely transmogrified" that "my dear old mother would never know me" (Plate 4:2).

On 6 January—in the company of two armed guards—Roberts tested his disguise. No one paid him any undue attention, but he quickly found that his garments were only a screen, and that his actions could easily give away his identity. While visiting the Mosque of Sultan al-Ghuri, Roberts was curious about a group of men working on a magnificently embroidered silk cloth. One of his guards informed him that it was a sacred drape made for the tomb of the prophet in Medina. A group of pilgrims was getting ready to make the journey to deliver it. Roberts drew near the circle and imitated the others who knelt before it. But when he did, the gathering of men fell silent. Roberts had made a mistake; the others had kissed the cloth, but he had only examined it. One of his guards quickly signaled him—lifting a finger to his lips and then drawing it across his throat—and Roberts knelt a second time, and then quickly backed away. That night he wrote in his journal: "It makes my hair stand on end to think what terrifying punishment would have been inflicted on me for my involuntary crime if it had become known that the sacred drapery had been contaminated by the touch of an infidel." Roberts quickly learned to observe and think before he acted, and his error was not repeated.

Great ceremony surrounded the departure of the pilgrims to Medina, and, for several days, Roberts's attention was riveted on their preparations. On 8 January, the pilgrims gathered on the square in front of the main entrance to the Citadel. Roberts sketched the activity in detail, noting the assembly of the caravan and its camels, the elegant dress of the pilgrims, arrayed in jewel-bright striped caftans, as well as the crowds who gathered to wish the pilgrims a safe journey. He later combined his observations into a panoramic scene,

Plate 4:3   *Citadel of Cairo, Residence of Mehemet Ali.* From *Egypt and Nubia* (London: F. G. Moon, 1846–1849). Library of Congress, Washington, D.C.

depicting the caravan taking the sacred drape out of the precincts of Cairo, with a broad vista of the Citadel behind them (Plate 4:3).

On 13 January, in the company of Louis Linant, his acquaintance from Alexandria, and John Pell, a new friend he had made in Cairo, Roberts rode into the desert, where groups from other regions of Egypt and from Constantinople had converged to join the pilgrimage. To Roberts's eye it was an unparalleled spectacle. Thousands of camels and hundreds of horses joined the throng that surrounded the tent of the emir where the prophet's cloth was protected. At midday, after morning prayers, a gunshot rang over the noise of the crowd, and the vast assembly rose as one and departed. For Roberts, the great caravan, transporting its sacred gift, evoked an image of "the children of Israel bearing the ark through the wilderness." But the grand display—"the rich trappings and gay coverings of the tents born on the backs of camels"—dispelled the aura of solemnity, suggesting instead that the pilgrimage was a celebratory occasion. For once, Roberts felt daunted as an artist: "I had my sketch-book, but there was so much to see that I could do little work."

Roberts also used his time in Cairo to return to Gizeh, to sketch the best-known monuments of ancient Egypt. His first glimpse of the pyramids on 3 October had been tinged with disappointment at their scale, but having seen the gigantic ruins of Karnak and Abu Simbel, Roberts developed a more subtle appreciation. He saw in them a poignant grandeur, commemorating a lost civilization whose achievements still elicited the admiration of the contemporary world. Roberts now regarded the pyramids in the light of "melancholy reflections," indicative of the "instability of all human greatness." On 17 January, he made three sketches of the pyramids, and from these he created a panoramic vista, adopting a high point of view (Plate 4:4). The striated structures rise out of the vast plain as if they were part of the natural setting. Other remnants of the once-grand site—a mastaba on the left and the Sphinx, half buried in sand, on the right—seem insignificant by comparison. Roberts added a group of Arabic men in the central foreground for visual interest, but a tiny figure, standing on an outcrop of rock to the right, seems to express his own personal sentiment, opening his arms, as if awestruck by the wonders before him.

As on his earlier visit, Roberts was enchanted by the Sphinx, the guardian figure of the Pyramid of Chefren, and he sketched it from several angles. Only the head was visible — drifting sand covered the leonine body — but Roberts chose a very low point of view to give the monument height and grandeur. In his lithograph design of the Great Sphinx, Roberts positioned members of a caravan in the purple shadows cast by the towering figure, enjoying some relief from the burning sun (Plate 4:5).

Roberts also used the Sphinx in a more fantastic context, as the centerpiece for the coming of the simoon, the harsh, burning wind that swept in from the southwest across the desert plains in early spring. In the text that accompanied Roberts's lithographs, William Brockedon compared it to the sirocco winds and called it "the fearful scourge to the traveller in the East." Laden

Plate 4:4 *Pyramids of Geezeh (Gizeh)*. From *Egypt and Nubia* (London: F. G. Moon, 1846–1849). Library of Congress, Washington, D.C.

Plate 4:5 *The Great Sphinx, Pyramids of Geezeh (Gizeh)*. From *Egypt and Nubia* (London: F. G. Moon, 1846–1849). Library of Congress, Washington, D.C.

Plate 4:6   *Approach of the Simoon.* From *Egypt and Nubia* (London: F.G. Moon, 1846–1849). Library of Congress, Washington, D.C.

Plate 4:7 *The Holy Tree, Metereah.*
From *Egypt and Nubia* (London:
F. G. Moon, 1846–1849). Library
of Congress, Washington, D.C.

with sand, the simoon clouded the atmosphere, and its burning winds, with their sulfurous smell, were believed to carry disease. Brockedon quoted a traveler named Bruce, who claimed that the heat of the simoon was like an oven's blast and that its force had knocked his party to its knees, leaving them too weak even to pitch their tents. Although Roberts did not experience the brutal winds, he constructed a vivid spectacle of their onslaught (Plate 4:6). In the sand-choked atmosphere, members of a caravan struggle against the mounting gusts, their garments whipping around them. At the far right, a tent is ripped from its pegs, and the camels resist their tenders who try to make them rise and leave the camp before the simoon attains its full force. Roberts could not resist the theatrical potential of his subject, and he sacrificed accuracy for drama. By changing the direction the Sphinx faced from east to west, he made it an emblem of endurance, staring bravely into the illumination of a blood-red setting sun.

One of Roberts's last sketching tours out of Cairo took him on 20 January to the Holy Tree of Metereah, a site popular with Christian pilgrims for many centuries (Plate 4:7). Legend associated the massive old sycamore with Joseph and Mary's flight from Bethlehem into Egypt to save their son from Herod's persecution. Exhausted from their journey, the Holy Family rested beneath the tree's twisting branches. Another tradition attributed a miracle to the site. There had been a fountain at the base of the tree, but the water it produced was so salty that it was not fit to drink. After the Virgin and Her Child sheltered there, the water became pure, sweet, and refreshing. Even during Roberts's day, the age of the tree was in doubt; one generation later,

Karl Baedeker's guide *Lower Egypt with the Fan and the Peninsula of Sinai* (1878) would claim it had been planted in 1672. Still, tourists flocked to the old sycamore, revering its role in Christian tradition and carving their names on the trunk as witness to their visit. Although Roberts always decried the practice of defacing monuments, like the others, he carved his name in the bark and cut off a small branch to bring to his daughter. He also made a sketch of the tree. Its thick, knotted branches seem to testify to its ancient significance, and the figures beneath it, dressed in flowing caftans—suggestive of biblical robes—give the scene the quality of timelessness.

For Roberts, the days spent sketching in and around Cairo provided a sense of satisfied productivity as well as a welcome distraction from the challenges of preparing for his upcoming expedition through Palestine and Syria. He waited anxiously for the documents he needed for the trip. He also worried about his finances, fearing that he did not have the funds to cover the great expense of hiring guides, transport animals, and equipment. Given the more arduous nature of the overland journey into less-traveled regions, Roberts was hesitant to make the trip on his own. He considered an invitation from his new friends in Cairo, John Pell and John Kinnear, the son of an Edinburgh banker, to join their entourage. Pell and Kinnear were less interested in biblical sites; they planned to travel to Petra, which did not figure in Roberts's itinerary. Roberts shared their desire to see the Monastery of Saint Catherine in the Sinai, but still he hesitated, eager to cross Syria and reach Jerusalem by the most direct route.

With his usual good fortune—and his willingness to take advantage of unexpected opportunities—Roberts found the solutions he sought. On 12 January, while sketching in the inner courtyard of the Mosque of Sultan Hassan, he struck up a conversation with a young Turk who had been watching him work. Haafee Ismail Effendi spoke fluent English, and Roberts discovered to his surprise that the young man was a Christian, baptized in Glasgow and educated in Europe. Effendi now served as a member of the pasha's entourage. They became fast friends, and when Roberts invited Effendi to join him on his journey, the Turk happily accepted. Similarly, Roberts's anticipated financial problems disappeared when Robert Thorburn, the vice-consul in Alexandria, sent him a loan of forty pounds.

Warned of the dangers of traveling through desolate areas, where travelers were often attacked by bandits and animals or detained by hostile agents of local sheiks, Roberts reluctantly bought an arsenal of rifles, pistols, and sabers. He intended to make the journey in his Turkish garb, and he grew a thick mustache to further alter his Western appearance. But on 21 January, after he had hired four camels for the expedition, he received distressing news. Reports of plague in the vicinity of Jerusalem prompted local authorities to place the region under a cordon sanitaire; no one would be allowed to enter or leave the area until it was lifted. Roberts's friends in the foreign office were powerless to help him, and he wrote of his frustration in his journal: "This annoyed me very much. To visit Syria without seeing Jerusalem would be as bad as to visit England without seeing London." Roberts spent his days nervously awaiting bulletins about the status of the quarantine. For distraction, he turned his attention to making a panorama of Cairo, which he planned to send to his friend Robert Burford, the proprietor of two specialty theaters in London, one on the Strand and one in Leicester Square. In his typical modest self-assessment, he concluded that the finished work—four and a half sheets showing a full view of the cityscape—was "not bad work for the time; the subject is excellent."

On 28 January, Roberts was informed by the British foreign office that the news from Jerusalem had been in error. There was no cordon sanitaire, no evidence of plague; Jerusalem was accessible to travelers. Relieved—and eager to start his journey—Roberts and Effendi agreed to join Pell and Kinnear on a route that would include Mount Sinai, Petra, Hebron, and Jerusalem. They set their departure for the following week. The next day, Roberts received letters of introduction to the consuls in Jerusalem and Damascus from Colonel Campbell, as well as a firman signed by Pasha Mehemet Ali. His set of documents was now complete. Roberts, Pell, and Kinnear celebrated their upcoming journey with a dinner hosted by Pell. The men ate "Turkish style," using fingers instead of forks, while dancing girls and musicians provided entertainment (Plate 4:8). In the following days, Roberts attended to final details, and on 31 January, he wrote his last letter from Cairo to his daughter, Christine: "I set out with two gentlemen, on the 6th of February for Syria, the most interesting country on the face of the earth, the scene of our Saviour's sufferings." For Roberts, navigating the Nile had been a romantic adventure and his interlude in Cairo a pleasant revelation, but headed for the Holy Land he recognized that the unpredictable route before him would constitute a journey of a very different nature.

Plate 4:8 *Dancing Girls at Cairo.* From *Egypt and Nubia* (London: F. G. Moon, 1846–1849). Library of Congress, Washington, D.C.

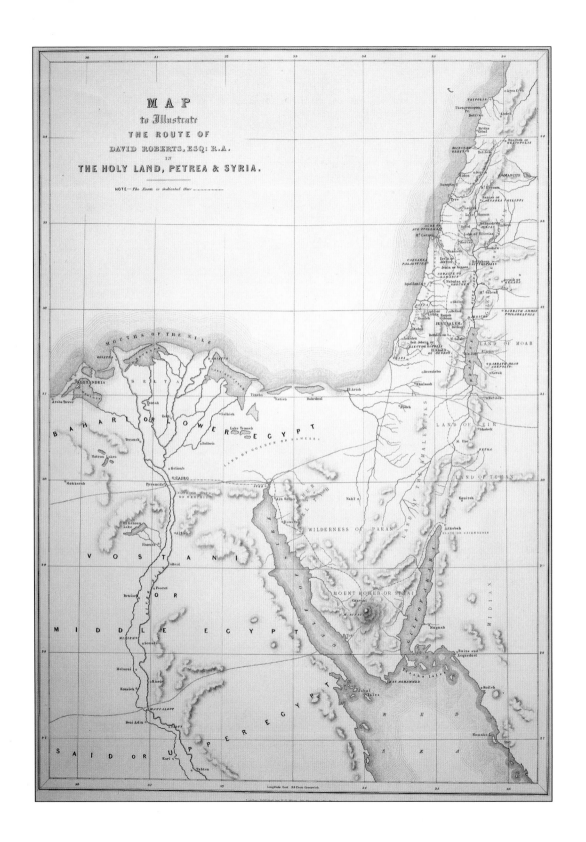

MAP
to Illustrate
THE ROUTE OF
DAVID ROBERTS, ESQ: R.A.
IN
THE HOLY LAND, PETREA & SYRIA.

NOTE—The Route is indicated thus ....

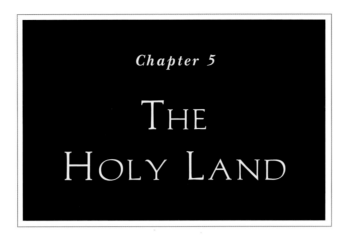

Chapter 5

THE HOLY LAND

ROBERTS AND HIS COMPANIONS SET OUT from Cairo with all the trappings of a traditional caravan. The British men wore Turkish costume, not only for comfort and protection against the heat and wind but also to disguise their foreign appearance. They rode camels rather than horses; they also used them—as well as donkeys—to transport their ample provisions. Along with tents, food, water, and utensils, they carried the arms that Roberts had purchased. Like their garments, these rifles, pistols, and sabers were as much for appearance as for ready protection. A Bedouin escort of fifteen men and twenty-one camels completed the party. Led by Sheik Hussein, from the Beni Said tribe, they would act as scouts, guides, negotiators, and—if necessary—bodyguards on the first leg of the journey across the Sinai desert. The route they followed had traditional associations: for Christians it was a holy route, the one used by Moses to lead the Israelites from Egypt to the Promised Land (Plate 5:1).

But the rugged reality of overland travel quickly dampened the romantic fantasy of Oriental adventure. On 7 February, one day's travel from Cairo, Roberts and his friends spent the first of countless nights sleeping on the hard desert ground, battered by cold, sand-laden winds. Their tents provided some protection, but sporadic rainstorms, such as the one on the night of 9 February, often made it impossible to pitch camp before their equipment was soaked and of little use. They met few other travelers on their route, and the grim, barren landscape was monotonous and desolate. On 10 February, Roberts noted in his journal the macabre quality of the arid terrain: "A desert—not a shrub or tree in the whole line of road, marked only by mouldering skeletons." In his account of the expedition, John Kinnear described the haunting sensation of rarely seeing another traveler on the road: a "ghastly and almost unearthly desolation."

Roberts rapidly adapted to a daily routine. The company would rise at dawn to break camp. Pausing only for a cup of strong coffee, the men would proceed on their route for about two hours, taking advantage of the low light and cool air before stopping for breakfast. They ate a hearty meal: remnants of the meat from the previous night's dinner, supplemented with dried fruit and bread. This, along with water carried in leather bottles—sometimes strengthened with a few drops of brandy—held the travelers until they camped for the night. Roberts recalled these simple meals with pleasure, claiming he ate them with "a gusto I have not experienced since boyhood."

Plate 5:1 *Map to Illustrate the Route of David Roberts, Esq: R. A. in the Holy Land, Petra & Syria.*
From *The Holy Land, Syria, Idumea, Arabia* (London: F. G. Moon, 1842). Newberry Library, Chicago.

Each day's travel was long—up to ten or twelve hours—with the caravan moving at a moderate pace. Roberts and Kinnear, both raised on long hikes through the highlands of their native Scotland, often walked well ahead of the party, preferring a more rapid gait.

Roberts soon discovered that the rigors of the journey demanded that he modify his working habits. The Nile cruise had allowed him to experience the sensations of the alien landscape before he put paper to pencil; now he had to work from his immediate impressions. Cairo's diversity had been a source of inspiration, but the desert crossing was barren, empty of stimulating visual variety. The route also posed an artistic challenge; the arid land they traversed lacked the architectural monuments that so often formed the central subject of his views. Undaunted, Roberts turned his attention to his own companions. On 12 February, he commented in his journal, "Our camels, Arabs, tents, and baggage lie scattered about in the way an artist likes." The word he used most often to describe the scene was "picturesque," referring not just to the exotic quality of his caravan but also to the term's essential meaning: these scenes provided perfect subjects for pictures. But twelve-hour days left Roberts little time or energy to sketch. Although he delighted in the sight of "our Bedouin Arabs at night as they gather around the fire," he regretted that "thirty miles a-day, sitting on a camel, rather unfits me for sketching them."

Sketching began in earnest when the party reached the Gulf of Suez three days after setting out from Cairo. Roberts sought to capture the striking contrast of the arid landscape and vivid atmospheric effects that characterized the region. Later, in the studio, the image of his first view across the gulf to the city provided a backdrop for his memories of his "picturesque" companions resting on the water's shore after the first arduous leg of their journey (Plate 5:2). He portrayed the members of the Bedouin escort in their distinctive garments: a short, white shirt with loose sleeves, made of coarse cotton, worn under a distinctive robe of striped wool. Their head covering—the kaffiyeh, a large square of cotton secured to the crown with a band of twisted worsted—protected them from the sun's burning rays and, when needed, screened their faces from the dust and wind. Turbans distinguished the men of higher rank. With rifles, hampers, bedrolls, and camels, the vignette suggests a typical evening after a long day's ride. In fact, Roberts and his British companions spent their nights in Suez in a hotel, another establishment run by the English-born proprietor Hill from Cairo.

A tone of reverence runs through Roberts's impressions of the lands along his route. Unlike the Nile journey, where his landmarks were the ancient ruins of a lost civilization now being uncovered by modern archaeological science, his progress through the Holy Land held a personal significance. Strong in his Protestant beliefs, Roberts saw each historic site as a confirmation of the foundations of his religion. While ruins traditionally signified the passage of human glory, the region he traversed was, for the most part, devoid of ruins. Barren and still, the land bore timeless witness to the episodes of faith that, in Roberts's mind, were greater than any other actions in human history. Gazing across the Suez, he was moved by the stark beauty of "the

SUEZ. *Feby 11th 1839*

Plate 5:2   *Suez (General View)*. From *The Holy Land, Syria, Idumea, Arabia* (London: F. G. Moon, 1842). Newberry Library, Chicago.

Plate 5:3 *Approach to Mount Sinai, Wady Baráh.* From *The Holy Land, Syria, Idumea, Arabia* (London: F. G. Moon, 1842). Library of Congress, Washington, D.C.

mountains . . . reflecting the setting sun, in a red glow of fire, contrasting powerfully with the deep blue sea," but beyond its physical beauty, he saw in the vista a "moral grandeur" derived from "the mighty events which took place there." Each stage of the journey was defined by its association with biblical incident. Upon reaching the Red Sea on 12 February, he reflected that it held "ten-fold interest" in remembrance of the divine intervention that had allowed Moses to part the waters and lead his followers to safety. Three days later, after a fifteen-hour trek through the "wilderness of Sinai," his own travails seemed light when compared to those of the Israelites, who "were condemned to wander for forty years" (Plate 5:3).

On the night of 18 February, after a gloomy three-hour journey ascending a mountain path, Roberts and his company reached the ancient Monastery of Saint Catherine. The religious community there traced its foundations to the early fourth century, when Queen Helena, the mother of the Roman Emperor Constantine, had made a pilgrimage through the region, visiting holy sites. At Mount Sinai, she had determined the exact location of the Burning Bush, in which an angel had appeared to Moses as divine affirmation. To commemorate her discovery, Helena had a small chapel built on the site and dedicated it to the Virgin. Within a few years, a monastic community had grown up around it. Through the centuries, the monks remained there, their monastery surviving as a Christian enclave during the Islamic conversion of the region and as a sanctuary for old practices and revered objects when the Byzantine Emperor Leo III, spurred by the

iconoclasts, ordered the destruction of all sacred imagery in 726. Isolation had been the key to the monastery's survival, and over a thousand years later, it endured, nestled in the steep cliffs like a fortress, safe behind impenetrable walls of hewn granite.

The travelers were exhausted by their perilous climb on a road blocked by rubble that had tumbled from the retaining walls. When they reached their destination, it proved difficult to attract the attention of the residents in the monastery. Repeated shouts finally brought forth some monks with torches to guide the men into the enclave. Even their entry was rough. There was no direct path into the monastery; a stout rope was dropped from a cabin above the narrow passage, and members of Roberts's party were hauled up, one by one, with the rope secured around their waists. They were then led through a maze of dimly lit corridors to be presented to the abbot, who welcomed them with a modest dinner of rice and dried dates and gave them rooms to shelter them for the length of their stay. Roberts wrote in his journal: "Never did poor pilgrim sleep more soundly than I did under the hospitable roof of the monks of St. Catherine."

At daylight, Roberts was astonished at the vitality of the monastic community. Within the walls was a small but lively town, complete and thoroughly self-sufficient (Plate 5:4). He also observed a rare harmony between two faiths that had long existed in opposition, for in addition to the magnificent Church of the Transfiguration, founded by Emperor Justinian in 530, and the ancient

Chapel of the Burning Bush, the enclave protected a mosque, built by the Prophet Muhammad. For several days, Roberts and his companions accepted the monks' simple but generous hospitality, making daily expeditions to the surrounding holy sites and returning to the monastery each evening for shelter. On 20 February, they ascended Mount Horeb—the summit of the Sinai—up a treacherous path, relieved partly by the "Stairway of Moses," three hundred roughly cut granite slabs, said to be the work of a single monk's pious labor. Two chapels graced the summit: one commemorating the spot where Moses received the tablets of divine law and one built over the preserved footprint of the camel that had carried Muhammad on his journey from Sinai to Mecca. The sheer beauty of the vista from the summit touched Roberts deeply; he claimed it was "the most sublime that can be imagined." On 22 February, Roberts returned to Mount Horeb to draw the Rock of Moses, where water flowed to refresh the prophet and his followers, and, later that day, the traveling party left the monastery for Aqaba, its next destination heading toward the fabled city of Petra. The men expected the journey to Aqaba to take a day.

Within a few hours after their departure from the monastery, the travelers realized that they had severely miscalculated the time they needed to reach Aqaba. The roads were barely passable—steeper and in far worse condition than they had expected. On 24 February, after two days of rugged ten-hour journeys, Roberts and his party finally put the looming massif of the Sinai behind them. The terrain softened, and the gentler, rolling sand hills made their progress easier. Their day's journey concluded at the shores of the Gulf of Aqaba, where they camped near the clear, cooling water. But the following day they were pummeled by the hot southwesterly winds of the sirocco. Roberts compared the experience to "a hurricane, with dense clouds of sand, so that we could not see our way six yards before us." They sheltered for the night in a protected bay, revived somewhat by a dinner of freshly caught fish. But even at the shore the heat was oppressive. Although the winds abated the next day, the journey was miserable, for their miscalculation had left them with an insufficient supply of potable water.

At midday on 27 February, they reached the Fortress of Aqaba. They quenched their thirst and replenished their water supply, making camp outside the walls of the garrison. The governor came out to receive them and offer hospitality in the barracks, but, wary of the local customs, Roberts and his companions politely refused. They did accept refreshments of coffee and a pipe, and, during their conversation, the governor inquired about their plans. Upon hearing that they intended to travel to Petra to visit the ruins of the ancient city, he informed them that they could neither pass through the region nor stay at the site without permission of the Alloueen Bedouins, who held regional authority over Wadi Mousa, the settlement nearest Petra. The sheik of the Alloueen Bedouins was summoned to the fortress, but it took three days for him to arrive. Roberts and his party took advantage of the delay to rest from their exhausting journey. On 2 March, when they at last sat down with the tribal leader, they were confronted with new unforeseen obstacles to

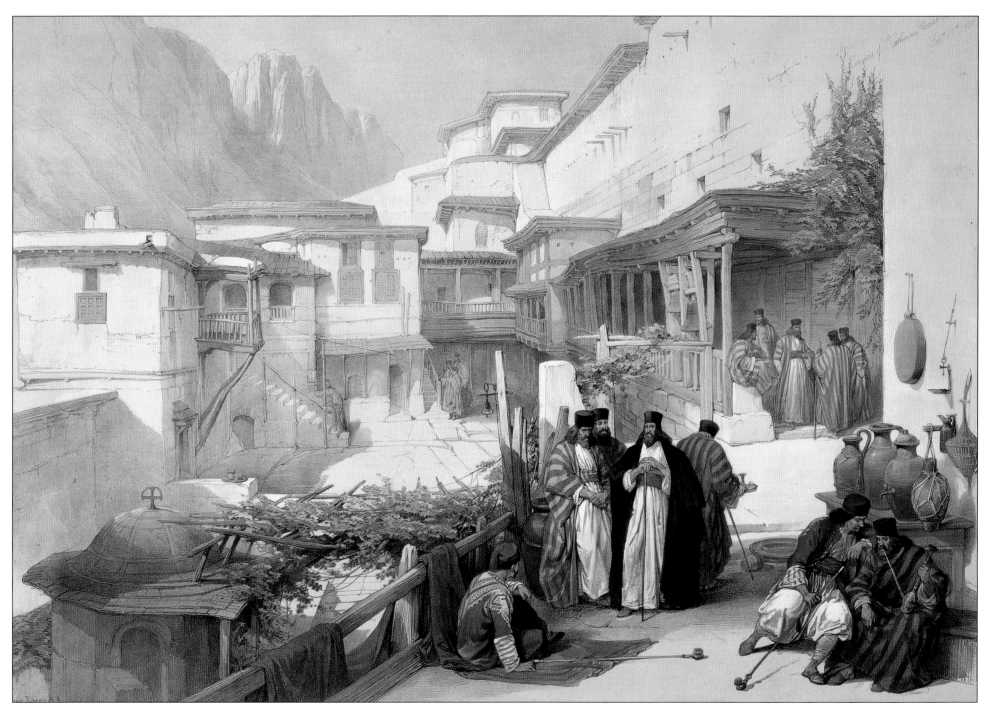

Plate 5:4 *Convent of Saint Catherine, Mount Sinai.* From *The Holy Land, Syria, Idumea, Arabia* (London: F. G. Moon, 1842). Library of Congress, Washington, D.C.

Plate 5:5 *Entrance to Petra.* From *The Holy Land, Syria, Idumea, Arabia* (London: F. G. Moon, 1842). Library of Congress, Washington, D.C.

their plans. Roberts described their negotiations as a "grand palaver," and, "after much beating around the bush," the parties agreed upon terms. The Beni Said escort was dismissed, replaced by a party of Alloueens. The sheik would travel with them, and Roberts would pay a fee of forty-five hundred piastres—roughly forty-five pounds—for escorted passage and the privilege of exploring the monuments of Petra without restriction.

The newly formed caravan left Aqaba on the morning of 3 March in a heavy mist, which Roberts claimed made the desert look "more dreary than usual." Two days later, the men pitched their tents at Wadi Mousa, in the shadow of the red sandstone cliffs that surrounded Petra. Roberts could not contain his eagerness: "Anxious to get a glimpse of Petra, I ascended the mountain and found another hill intervened, but the view of the Valley forming the ancient bed of the Jordan was magnificent."

In Roberts's day, few western travelers made the journey to Petra, and little was known of the site outside the region. Even today, historians are uncertain when the nomadic Nabateans made their way from Palestine into the deep, arid canyon, but by the first century B.C., they had built a magnificent capital with grand edifices hewn into the face of the roseate cliffs. In the ancient world, Petra stood at the crossroads of trade routes, which brought great wealth into the settlement. It eventually grew to a grand metropolis of thirty thousand inhabitants covering four hundred square miles. In addition to trade and architecture, the Nabateans demonstrated a genius for hydraulics, storing and circulating water in a system that made extraordinary use of the limited local rainfall, less than six inches per year. The Nabateans benefited from the decline of Greek power in the area, but in 106 A.D. they were dominated by Roman forces. To subjugate the territory to Roman rule, caravan trade was rerouted to bypass Petra. A series of earthquakes rocked the city between the fourth and sixth centuries, and by the seventh century the city was abandoned, with layer upon layer of debris and sand building up around the magnificent ruins. In the West, Petra had been known through legend more than history until the Swiss archaeologist Johann Burckhardt visited it in 1812, disguised as a Muslim pilgrim en route to Mecca.

At dawn on 6 March, Roberts and his party prepared to climb the final ascent that led to the ravine trails into Petra (Plate 5:5). The sheik tried to persuade Roberts to leave the camels and their equipment in Wadi Mousa and return that night to camp, but Roberts refused, fearing perhaps that his access to the city would be further limited. At the top of the precipice, with the canyon below them, Roberts and his companions were surrounded by another group of Bedouins, the Felloueens, who claimed that the Alloueens had no jurisdiction over the precincts of Petra. New negotiations were conducted, and Roberts was forced to pay an additional fee of three hundred piastres for the privilege of remaining in the ruined city for five days. It was less time than Roberts had wanted. When the caravan descended into the canyon and camped in the shadow of the rock-cut ruins, he quickly surveyed the site and began to sketch.

Petra amazed him. On 9 March he wrote: "I am more and more astonished and bewildered with this extraordinary city." The array of buildings was grander and more diverse than he had imagined, and he was hard put to characterize the architectural style, which seemed to him a conflation of Egyptian form with Greek and Roman decoration. Roberts worked as quickly as he was able, drawing the amphitheater—originally built by the Nabateans and expanded by the Romans—and the buildings called "The Mansions" and El Deir ("The Monastery"). The actual functions of many of the buildings are still in question. To Roberts's eye, El Khasneh ("The Treasury") was the most spectacular and best-preserved facade (Plate 5:6). On either side of the projecting portal, with its pediment supported by colossal Corinthian columns, were the remnants of a sculpted frieze, featuring heroically proportioned equestrians in the Hellenistic style. The tholos on the second level, set into a square formed by semi-pediments, also bore witness to classical influence in its elaborate decorative details and the lithe female figures presiding in niches defined by embedded columns. Perhaps thinking of the splendor of Egyptian monuments, Roberts believed that the building was a mausoleum, but Bedouin legend held that the wealth of ancient Petra had been safeguarded within the rock-hewn chambers behind the facade, giving the structure its name.

Roberts's time at Petra passed quickly; on one day he was impeded by heavy rain, although he kept sketching despite the downpour. On 11 March, the last day of his authorized stay, he was roused from sleep before dawn by

Plate 5:6 *Petra (El Khasneh)*. From
The Holy Land, Syria, Idumea, Arabia
(London: F. G. Moon, 1842). Library
of Congress, Washington, D.C.

a disturbance in camp. A robber had ransacked the tent shared by Pell and Effendi, making off with a brace of pistols and a bag of percussion caps. Pell caught sight of the intruder as he escaped under a side of the tent but was not alert enough to pursue him. The caravan packed its belongings and made its way out of the canyon, where the strange turn of events left Roberts in a pensive mood. He wrote: "At 8 the camels were loaded, and I repeatedly turned back to look at the deserted city, so sad a memorial of divine judgment. In its strength it must have scorned all human means of destruction, for in comparison, all walls built by man were insignificant."

The caravan headed north, once again moving slowly through the rugged terrain. On 16 March, Hebron, one of the oldest cities of Judea, appeared on the horizon. Surrounded by walls constructed in the reign of Herod, it nestled in a range of rolling hills covered with olive trees and vines. Roberts saw it as an oasis, curiously reminiscent of home, in the unrelenting monotony of the landscape. He recorded his impressions in his journal: "On turning round the side of a hill, Hebron first bursts upon you. The situation is beautiful, and the houses, gleaming brightly in the noonday sun, reminded me of England." Even the children, who came out of the city to greet the caravan, "healthy and pretty" with "blooming countenances," raised his spirits after his grueling ride.

But Hebron presented new difficulties. Roberts was denied permission to sketch in the mosque that held the tombs of Abraham, Isaac, and Jacob. He confined his sketching to general views of the city. He and his companions did find hospitality, welcomed into the home of a man named Elias, the head of the only Christian family living in Hebron. Elias also had family in Jerusalem, but he informed Roberts that the city was under quarantine. The first rumor Roberts had heard in Cairo was, in fact, true. An outbreak of plague had occurred in Jerusalem, and all travelers were barred from entry. Dismayed but undaunted, Roberts and his party departed Hebron for Gaza on 18 March. They reached their destination in two days and remained in Gaza until 23 March, replenishing their provisions and purchasing additional camels. Two days later they arrived at Jaffa. Surrounded by orange groves and rising on a hill that slopes gently to the sea shore, Jaffa was beautiful from a distance, but, upon entering the city, Roberts sadly saw that the population had been devastated by disease and that those who survived lived in poverty. On 26 March, John Kinnear left the caravan to take a more direct route to Beirut, where he needed to attend to family business. Roberts, Pell, and Effendi continued on toward Jerusalem, traveling now with only three servants and eight horses to carry their equipment.

On the evening of 28 March, Roberts and his companions approached the outskirts of Jerusalem and set up camp within a reasonable distance of the city walls, wondering if it was practical to wait for the quarantine to be lifted. There was no indication of life within the city. Roberts slept poorly. The night's disturbing silence was broken sporadically by the howl of a dog and the screech of an owl. The next morning, his fortunes changed, prompting him to write in his journal "It is better to be born lucky than rich." Throngs of people—soldiers beating drums and waving banners, women and children singing and dancing—spilled out of the city gate. From every direction, crowds of pilgrims converged on the city. It was the first day of Holy Week, and the quarantine had been lifted. There were now so many visitors to Jerusalem that Roberts and his friends were unable to find hotel accommodations, but in Hebron, Elias had urged them to contact his family if they found themselves in need of hospitality, and they were welcomed in like old friends.

Roberts promptly made a preliminary tour of the city, selecting the subjects he wanted to sketch. At every turn he was surrounded by crowds of pilgrims who filled the narrow streets. In the courtyard in front of the Church of the Holy Sepulchre, he saw with delight a bustling bazaar selling crosses, rosaries, staffs, and relics to the celebrants. Roberts was amazed to see Greek pilgrims, barefoot on prayer rugs, making their devotions in the open air as they stood on a terrace facing the Holy Sepulchre, with the pool of Bethesda behind them and the grand dome of the Mosque of Omar in the distance (Plate 5:7). He had not experienced such vitality and diversity since leaving Cairo.

On 30 March, Roberts met with Achmed Aga, the governor of Jerusalem, who generously offered to help him in every way possible. Achmed provided a room with excellent views of the city in which Roberts could work and an escort through the crowded streets. Upon hearing that Roberts planned to travel to Jericho, the governor declared that he personally intended to escort a group of pilgrims to the banks of the Jordan, and he invited Roberts to join the official party. When Roberts expressed his gratitude for such a warm and generous reception, Achmed Aga modestly deferred to the policies of Mehemet Ali, claiming that every letter he received from the pasha directed him to be kind to European visitors.

Roberts spent most of the following morning—Palm Sunday—in the Greek Chapel of the Holy Sepulchre (Plate 5:8). He witnessed an extraordinary procession of priests and pilgrims from every region of the Christian world. The first group to enter represented the Greek Orthodox faith. Led by a party of bishops, they wore richly embroidered vestments, waved painted banners, and circled the sepulchre three times, pausing for the pilgrims to kneel and kiss the crucifix carried at the head of the procession. A group of Armenian priests followed, then Syrians and Coptic Christians, who seemed to Roberts impoverished by comparison, carrying staffs of ivory rather than gold. In the text for *The Holy Land*, George Croly reported that Roberts saw "costumes and countenances from all parts of the world; the splendid robes and dark visages of the Asiatic, the powerful features of the Greek, the Italian monk, the Syrian mountaineer, the Christian of India, some countenances wild and barbarian, some brilliant and civilized . . . a vast congregation gathered by one powerful impulse to do homage to the most awful place of recollection on the globe."

Plate 5:7 *The Mosque of Omar.* From *The Holy Land, Syria, Idumea, Arabia* (London: F. G. Moon, 1842). Library of Congress, Washington, D.C.

Plate 5:8   *The Shrine of the Holy Sepulchre.* From *The Holy Land, Syria, Idumea, Arabia* (London: F.G. Moon, 1842). Library of Congress, Washington, D.C.

For his week-long journey to Jericho, Roberts traveled lightly, taking only his tent, his portfolio, and one servant. He left at dawn on 1 April, riding through the Valley of Jehoshaphat to the foothills of the Mount of Olives. He stayed in Bethany long enough to make a few sketches and then descended into the Valley of the Jordan, where Achmed Aga and four thousand pilgrims made their camp. Well before dawn, a shot rang out over the encampment, signaling that the governor and his party were ready to depart. Roberts hurried to catch up to the caravan, which stretched as far as the eye could see. The travelers moved in solemn silence, but, when they reached the banks of the river, the procession dissolved into what Roberts perceived as pandemonium. "A general rush took place, and the women broke into the shrill cry of joy so often heard in Egypt." From the comfort of carpets spread by the governor's party on a rise above the river, Roberts was flabbergasted to see the pilgrims strip off their clothing and plunge into the waters of the Jordan River (Plate 5:9). "The scene was most exciting. Young and old, male and female, were in the stream in one promiscuous mass—some nude, some slightly dressed." Garments that were saturated with the water were regarded as sacred; they would be worn again only as funeral shrouds. When Roberts learned that a young pilgrim from Greece had waded far into the currents of the rushing water and drowned, he reflected that "many others narrowly escaped the same fate."

The next day, after the governor's party had departed for Jerusalem, Roberts traveled on to the Dead Sea and the Greek Orthodox Monastery of Saint Saba. He made a brief visit to Bethlehem and then returned to Jerusalem. On 8 April, he reluctantly bid farewell to Pell and Effendi, who now planned to return to Cairo. During the next few days, Roberts sketched in the churches and shrines; he also traversed the outskirts of the city, drawing vistas of Jerusalem from the east, the south, and the north (Plate 5:10). Perhaps he had hoped to use the drawings for a panorama, but he lamented on 12 April, "I have wandered over the hills but have not been able to get a good view of the city." Three days later, he packed his equipment and headed north toward Lebanon for the last leg of his journey, looking forward to seeing the ruins of Baalbec and the city of Damascus.

During his first night on the trail, Roberts's tent was surrounded by jackals. They did no harm, but they seemed to portend a difficult journey ahead. En route from Nablus to Cana, the landscape was unrelentingly barren, but the revered sites of biblical history—at Samara the ancient synagogue, the well of Jacob, and the tombs of Joseph and his sons; at Nazareth the Grotto of the Annunciation, Joseph's workshop, and the Fountain of the Virgin—gave Roberts ample subjects to sketch (Plate 5:11). On 21 April, Roberts reached Cana, the sight of one of Christ's first miracles, changing water into wine.

Plate 5:9   *Banks of the River Jordan.* From *The Holy Land, Syria, Idumea, Arabia* (London: F. G. Moon, 1842). Library of Congress, Washington, D.C.

Plate 5:10 *Jerusalem*. From *The Holy Land, Syria, Idumea, Arabia* (London: F. G. Moon, 1842). Library of Congress, Washington, D.C.

Plate 5:11 *Nazareth (General View)*. From *The Holy Land, Syria, Idumea, Arabia* (London: F. G. Moon, 1842). Library of Congress, Washington, D.C.

Once a thriving city, Cana was now reduced to a poor village of no more than forty or fifty huts. Roberts stopped at a small Greek Orthodox church, where the priests displayed their treasured relic: the jar that had held the wine that Christ created for the wedding guests. After spending a few hours in the little town, Roberts moved on to the city of Tiberias, riding through more gentle and verdant land, passing the Sea of Galilee along the way.

Within a week, Roberts had reached Sidon, a city on the Mediterranean with the mountains of Lebanon looming behind. At the gates of the city, Roberts and his men were stopped by guards, who questioned them about the lands they had visited. Hearing that they had come from Palestine so soon after the quarantine had been lifted, the guards demanded to see health certificates. Unaware that he needed that particular document, Roberts thought quickly and flourished his firman bearing the pasha's signature, threatening that "if they stopped me they must be answerable for the consequences." The ruse worked, and a soldier was appointed as their personal escort in the city, but his presence made a spectacle of Roberts and his party. "Wherever we walked he preceded us, beating every one out of the way, and calling out we were in quarantine, till people actually believed we were plague subjects." Roberts managed to make only a few sketches of the ancient fort in Sidon, and, for two nights' duration, he and his men camped on the shore rather than trying to find accommodations under the bizarre circumstances (Plate 5:12).

On 29 April Roberts left Sidon. Travel through the increasingly rugged terrain slowed the party's progress, and Roberts complained in his journal of constant fatigue. Provisions were running low; the guard in Sidon, by branding them as quarantined, had made it impossible for them to purchase what they needed. Now, little was left in their packs. Roberts wrote that his troop was "in want of everything. Our light is from a bit of rag in a dish of butter; tea we have none; coffee, but no sugar. Wine and spirits have long been unknown; my only solace before turning into bed is a pipe of tobacco." The lands through which they passed were controlled by the Druse. Their beliefs and customs, which Roberts thought were neither Christian nor Moslem, were totally unknown to him or the members of his party. This added a sense of trepidation to the journey, and on 1 May, when they reached Zahleh, what they discovered gave them added reason to worry. Civil disturbance was expected to erupt in Baalbec. But Roberts was determined to finish his journey as planned, and, after a meeting with the local governor, he continued on, now in the company of three soldiers on horseback, heavily armed, with orders to guard the painter and his entourage.

Roberts and his party rode to the site of Baalbec on 2 May in a heavy rainstorm. He was miserable, totally drenched and feverish. But the sight of the ruins of the ancient Roman settlement rallied him. Despite his physical debilitation, "I was . . . so much struck with the magnificence of the temple, that I could not resist visiting and examining it" (Plate 5:13). The storm continued through the night, pummeling the tents. In the morning, Roberts felt extremely ill and sought the help of a Greek priest, who found him dry shelter in a cowshed. For the first time on his grueling journey, Roberts devoted the whole day to bed rest.

Plate 5:12   *Sidon (Looking towards Lebanon).* From *The Holy Land, Syria, Idumea, Arabia* (London: F. G. Moon, 1842). Library of Congress, Washington, D.C.

Plate 5:13 *Baalbec (Remains of the Western Portico)*. From *The Holy Land, Syria, Idumea, Arabia* (London: F. G. Moon, 1842). Newberry Library, Chicago.

Plate 5:15   *Baalbec (The Doorway)*. From
The Holy Land, Syria, Idumea, Arabia
(London: F. G. Moon, 1842).
Newberry Library, Chicago.

On 4 May, regaining some strength, Roberts explored the site. With obscure origins connected with the god Baal, the city of Baalbec had grown to importance in Hellenistic times, when it was known as Heliopolis ("City of the Sun"). In the first century B.C., the Romans had established a cult of the Heliopolitan Jupiter there, and both Josephus Flavius, in 64 B.C., and Strabo mention the city as a center for worship of the solar incarnation of the head deity of their pantheon. The city remained prominent through the seventh century, when the Arab residents of Baalbec turned the temples into fortresses. Conquered by Saladin and plundered by Tamerlane, the city saw its glory finally reduced to rubble in a series of earthquakes in the seventeenth and eighteenth centuries. But what remained on the site testified to Baalbec's former grandeur. Roberts marveled at the mastery of Roman architects and masons, claiming that their stones were cut and laid with such accuracy that mortar was not needed. Despite his ill health, Roberts worked for four days, finding the grand ruins of Baalbec as wondrous as anything he had seen along the Nile (Plate 5:14).

The threat of insurrection persisted throughout Roberts's stay at Baalbec. On 5 May, he returned to his camp to find that the local government had seized his mules to carry provisions to its troops. Once again, Roberts brandished his firman, but none of the authorities could read Turkish. After some consideration, the Druse governor granted him permission to visit Damascus, providing a guard for protection. But on 8 May, when Roberts finished his

Plate 5:15   David Wilkie, *His Highness Mehemet Ali, Pasha of Egypt*, 1841. Oil on wood, 24 x 20 in. (61 x 50.8 cm). Tate Gallery, London.

Plate 5:16 *Interview with the Viceroy of Egypt at His Palace, at Alexandria.* From *Egypt and Nubia* (London: F. G. Moon, 1846–1849). Library of Congress, Washington, D.C.

sketching at the site, he decided not to press his good fortune. Rather than journey into unstable territory, he headed for Beirut, where he would catch a steamer back to Alexandria. After two days' travel on rugged roads, he arrived in Beirut, which he declared to be "one of the prettiest towns in Syria." He called upon the British consul there and had a happy reunion with John Kinnear. On 13 May, he boarded a ship for the three-day journey to Alexandria.

Colonel Campbell met him at the dock. Roberts recalled the confusion of the first time he had pulled into the port of Alexandria and marveled that it now felt more familiar than exotic. Once again, he had little time to rest; on the following day, Campbell had arranged for the artist to be received by the pasha. The audience was brief, no more than twenty minutes, and Roberts was not allowed to sketch in Mehemet Ali's presence. He later regretted not bringing in his drawing materials, for he believed that he could have sketched the pasha's "animated countenance" without being seen. Two years later, Roberts's friend David Wilkie would be granted permission to paint the pasha's portrait (Plate 5:15), but Roberts had to content himself with reconstructing the scene from memory (Plate 5:16). He positioned himself leaning slightly forward, with Campbell at his right.

On 18 May, Roberts boarded a steamer for Malta. He had hoped for a rapid return, but a three-week-long quarantine, as well as visits with friends in Gibraltar and Cadiz, stretched the homebound journey to more than two months. He arrived in London on 21 July. Unlike the British travelers who preceded him, Roberts brought back few souvenirs. Instead he carried the record of his careful observations—272 drawings, three bulging sketchbooks, and a panorama of Cairo—an unparalleled testament to travel that would shape the British vision of the Middle East for generations to come.

Roberts returned to London with a pressing priority: to find a publisher willing to produce a deluxe edition of his travel views. Prior to his departure, he had offered the right of first refusal to the Finden Brothers' publishing house, which had engraved the illustrations for John Murray's 1836 two-volume edition *Landscape Illustrations of the Bible*. Along with Turner and Stanfield, Roberts had contributed designs for that project, based on rough sketches made at famous sites by travelers to Palestine. Roberts believed that the authenticity he could bring with his own on-the-spot observations would appeal to the Finden Brothers, but they never responded to his offer. He next turned directly to John Murray, whose interest was sparked. But when Murray calculated the costs of publishing a series of folio albums with colored lithographic views—an outlay of ten thousand pounds (approximately three hundred fifty thousand dollars in today's currency)—he dismissed the venture as too expensive to risk. Roberts refused to even consider a more modest presentation. As he noted in a letter to his friend Robert Sconce in Malta, there were many publishers interested

Chapter 6

THE RICHEST FOLIOS THAT EVER LEFT THE EAST

in his work: "My Sketches in the East have taken the world of art here by Storm. I am besieged by Publishers—but am Stoic enough to reject them all." Roberts was willing to delay publication to preserve his own vision; he was firm in believing that he had assemble "one of the richest folios that ever left the east."

In February 1840, Roberts signed a contract with Francis Graham Moon. Experienced in the publication of lithography albums, Moon was intrigued by Roberts's proposal: two volumes on Palestine and two volumes on Egypt, each featuring 120 full-page lithographic illustrations, plus one volume on modern Cairo, featuring 60 full-page lithographic illustrations. Unlike the popular "view" books of the previous decade, this series would emphasize image over text, and Moon was willing to take the financial risk to set a new standard of artistic merit. He agreed to publish the views in a folio edition, acknowledging that the large scale would present the images to their best advantage. He promised to hire the finest lithographers and to insist that they meet Roberts's exacting standards and work

Plate 6:0   *The Palace of Westminster and Whitehall Terrace,* 1862. Sotheby's, London.

Plate 6:1   David O. Hill and Robert Adamson, *Photograph of David Roberts,* c. 1843–1848. Scottish National Portrait Gallery, Edinburgh.

closely with the artist to translate his sketches with expression and integrity. Moon also met Roberts's price: three thousand pounds for the use and the copyright of a new set of sketches, based on those he had made during his travels.

Both Moon and Roberts were shrewd but careful businessmen, and together they formulated a strategy to stimulate interest in the publication—and raise substantial capital—well before it appeared. As a first step, they organized a private view of the most impressive of Roberts's watercolors and drawings for a select audience: Queen Victoria, the Archbishop of Canterbury, the Archbishop of York, and the Bishop of London. Each of these esteemed guests signed up for a subscription to the forthcoming series, and the queen even lent her name to the endeavor, allowing Roberts to dedicate the first volumes to her. Roberts and Moon then mounted exhibitions of selected travel sketches in London, Edinburgh, and several other major cities throughout Great Britain. The press notices were invariably favorable, and subscriptions came pouring in. By May 1841, after a little more than a year's promotion, Moon had raised nearly double the amount Murray had estimated the project would require. It pleased Roberts that subscriptions from Edinburgh amounted to more than twelve hundred pounds, proportionally far greater than those from London.

Roberts's rising reputation fueled the effort. In February 1840, Robert Scott Lauder painted Roberts in his Turkish costume (see Plate 4:5), presenting

Plate 6:2 *Jerusalem from the Mount of Olives,* 1842. Norwich Castle Museum

him as a romantic figure, handsome and daring enough for any adventure. Busy in his own studio, Roberts turned to his Eastern sketchbooks to inspire enticing subjects for exhibition oils. He presented the first of these—*The Greek Church of the Nativity at Bethlehem* (now in the Paisley Art Gallery) and *Dromos, or Outer Court of the Great Temple at Edfu* (private collection)—at the summer exhibition of the Royal Academy in London. Throughout his career, he would continue to use his travel sketches for evocative ideas, painting a total of fifty-five oils of Eastern subjects, and debuting thirty-one of them at the Royal Academy of Art. In 1841, he enjoyed the dual prestige of being elected a Royal Academician and receiving his first commission from the queen, a painting of *The Bridge of Toledo* (Royal Collection). His painting *Jerusalem from the Mount of Olives* (Plate 6:2 shows the lithograph version) also won widespread critical acclaim in that year's Royal Academy exhibition. Subtitled "During Easter, Christian Pilgrims from all Parts of the East Assembling at Jerusalem," the large-scale, panoramic setting was so convincing that viewers felt they were actually there witnessing the pious spectacle. The critic for the *Literary Gazette*

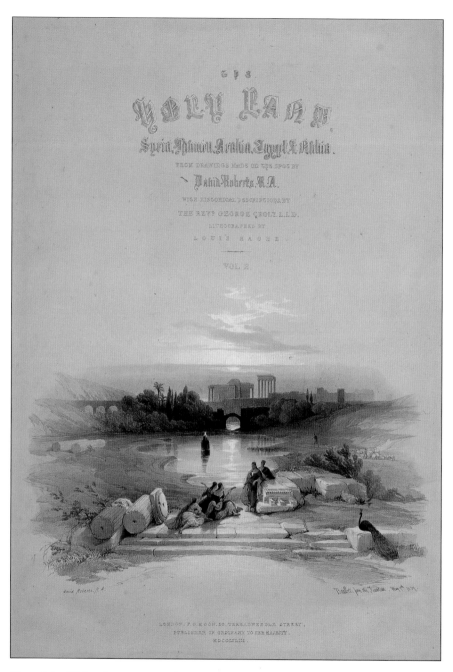

Plate 6:3 Title vignette to volume 1. From *The Holy Land, Syria, Idumea, Arabia* (London: F. G. Moon, 1842). Library of Congress, Washington, D.C.

praised Roberts's ability to "animate the canvass in a singularly effective manner, and impart to it a picturesqueness of infinite variety and beauty." Once again, Roberts entranced his audience with a combination of artistic skill and theatrical flair. He also used the opportunity to promote his planned publication. In the catalogue for the exhibition, he included the mournful opening meditation of the *Lamentations of Jeremiah:* "How doth the city sit in solitary that was full of people! How is she become a widow! She that was great among nations, and Prince among the provinces, how is she become tributary! Her gates are desolate. All her beauty is departed." The biblical quotation gave dramatic power to the picture, stirring religious feelings, while evoking a sense of the lost grandeur that once had graced the Orient. It was hardly a coincidence that Moon used the same quotation in the project prospectus.

In the early months of 1842, Roberts began the new sketches that would be used for the folios on Palestine and Syria. By the summer of 1844, he had completed 122 designs, working simultaneously on paintings for commissions and exhibition. Two years later, in the summer of 1846, he undertook the sketches for the folios on Egypt and Nubia, completing them in 1847. During this time, Moon hired writers to provide text for the publications; he chose two clergymen, George Croly for the Holy Land and William Brockedon for Egypt. To make the lithographic illustrations, he hired Louis Haghe. Born in Belgium, Haghe had learned the technique in Tournai, where he apprenticed with a French-trained master named Chevalier de la Barriere. In 1823, barely twenty years old, Haghe moved to London, finding a position with the printing firm of Day and Son, where he gained a reputation for having a fine touch and a subtle sense of color. Originally, Moon had planned to hire Haghe's brother Charles and several other lithographers to carry out the extensive series of illustrations. He also considered the services of J. D. Harding, a watercolorist and topographer, as a collaborator in the production. But Harding wanted to dominate the project, taking as his share all the large images and leaving Haghe with only the vignettes. Roberts intervened, and Harding was dropped. In the end, Haghe took on the full challenge of all the illustrations, much to Roberts's satisfaction. Roberts would later write in his journal "There can be only one opinion as to the masterly manner in which [Haghe] executed his work."

Individual folios of six illustrations with explanatory text were issued to subscribers as they were completed. The first folio of *The Holy Land* (Plate 6:3) appeared in April 1842; a total of twenty separate parts were issued to complete the ensemble over two years. Subscribers had the choice of hand-colored or uncolored—and therefore less expensive—editions. In November 1847, subscribers received the first folio of *Egypt and Nubia* (Plates 6:4 and 6:5). Issued in the same way, the publication of the whole project was completed by 1849. The finished work differed only slightly from Roberts's original plan. The complete opus, entitled *The Holy Land, Syria, Idumea, Arabia, Egypt, and Nubia*, was composed of two separate folio-sized editions—three volumes each—containing a total of 247 lithographs, two maps, the text, and a portrait of David Roberts (Plate 6:6).

Plate 6:4   Title vignette to volume 1. From *Egypt and Nubia* (London: F. G. Moon, 1846–1849). Library of Congress, Washington, D.C.

Plate 6:5   Title vignette to volume 2. From *Egypt and Nubia* (London: F. G. Moon, 1846–1849). Library of Congress, Washington, D.C.

The magnificent publication drew critical acclaim from all sectors of the art world. Recognized as unparalleled in quality—described by the critic in the *Art Union* as "a noble and beautiful work . . . foremost of the productions of the age and country"—*The Holy Land* was lauded for its scholarly contribution as well as its artistic merit. The reviewer in the *Athenaeum* praised it as "one of the most valuable publications of our day—vividly illustrating our readings in history, sacred as well as profane." The images of Palestine and Syria were of particular interest to the Victorian public; in these, Roberts documented the land on which sacred history had been enacted. Although he presented it as he had seen it—barren, arid, inhospitable—its association with the evangelical narratives of the Bible gave even the most desolate vista spiritual potency. In his text to *The Holy Land* Croly reflected: "Generations pass away, and the noblest monuments follow them; but the hills, the valley, and the stream exist, on which the eye of the Lord of all gazed; the soil on which his sacred footsteps trod; the magnificent landscape in the midst of which he lived." The rugged terrain of Roberts's renderings struck a note of reverence; as if enacting biblical prophecy, the land—now nearly devoid of life—testified to the frailty and vanity of human endeavor when weighed against divine intention.

Other, more affordable editions of Roberts's folios appeared, bringing his vision of the Middle East to an even wider audience. Shortly after the first sets were published, pirated editions were printed on the continent. To counter this, Moon supported an abbreviated French edition of sixty plates that was published in Brussels in 1843. Day and Sons—where Haghe was now a partner—brought out an octavo edition in black and white in 1856. An American edition—similarly more modest than the original—appeared in 1855, with a subsequent printing twenty-five years later. Roberts's Eastern views became a favored symbol for Western engagement with the distant Orient. Amateur archaeologists studied his renderings, regarding them as more accurate than those made by the French savants. Armchair travelers used the images to transport themselves on imaginary journeys to exotic destinations. And in his novel *Tancred, or the New Crusade* (1849), Benjamin Disraeli used Roberts's views as a symbol of his character's intellect, taste, and spiritual inclinations. Lord Montacute, the pious protagonist of the tale, gazes upon Roberts's lithographs to focus his devout meditations.

In the flattering light of success, Roberts retained his characteristic modesty. At a dinner held in his honor in Edinburgh on 19 October 1842, the presiding dignitary, Lord Henry Thomas Cockburn, called for a toast to Roberts, who had "completed the finest pilgrimage of art which has ever perhaps been performed by a single man." When praised for returning home "laden with the richest treasures," Roberts dismissed the high praise, pointing out that he had portrayed "a subject which—whoever had attempted it—would have brought fame." When an organization in Glasgow offered to host a similar dinner, Roberts politely refused.

Roberts never diminished the importance of Haghe's contribution to the project as a lithographer and colorist. The extent to which Roberts guided Haghe is not fully known. He did produce a new sketch for each print, and

Plate 6:6   C. Baugniet, *Portrait of David Roberts*, 1844. From *The Holy Land, Syria, Idumea, Arabia* (London: F. G. Moon, 1842) Library of Congress, Washington, D.C.

Plate 6:7 *Dendera*, 1848. Watercolor and bodycolor, 19 ¹⁄₈ x 13 ¹⁄₂ in. (48.6 x 34.3 cm). Aberdeen Art Gallery and Museum.

Haghe's reputation was built on his ability to translate an individual artist's distinctive style to the lithographic stone. To enhance the quality of drawing, Haghe worked his outlines in a soft gray and printed the image in two muted tones. The more vivid colors were added by hand, likely by a team of colorists working under Haghe's direction. The moody tonality and the expressive use of hue to evoke illumination, shadow, and atmosphere in the finished print fully echo Roberts's own use of color in his paintings, suggesting that Haghe strove to reproduce the artist's interpretation, as well as his image. In the course of the project, Haghe and Roberts developed a deep and enduring friendship; in the decade after the publication was completed they toured the continent together on several occasions.

Roberts was less content with the authors Moon had chosen for the text. Croly's essays for *The Holy Land* were heavily laden with scriptural quotations and the stern moral conviction that the region's desolation was a just example of divine judgment on human weakness. Roberts described Croly to his friend Hay as "An arrogant proud prelate who just writes and does as he likes with little regard to the subjects." On meeting him, Roberts's daughter, Christine, exclaimed: "He is even worse than I expected," and she believed him to be "the most bearish egotistical conceited person I ever met." As for his text, Roberts gave him a reserved endorsement noting, "it is at least equal to all that was expected of him." He held a lower opinion of Brockedon, who relied heavily on Roberts's own notes and was reticent to do his own research. Roberts complained to his son-in-law (Christine had married Henry Bicknell in 1841), "Indeed I question whether he has in all that is written given the *original idea*, let alone any original matter but what I have furnished him with. Now he must betake himself to read up a little." In the earliest stage of the project, Roberts's friend, the arts writer and poet Allan Cunningham, had asked Roberts to see whether he might be considered as an author, noting that while "the person who penned the letterpress should be familiar with Scripture and with eastern History," he also brought the perspective of "taste in art, and a knowledge of both sculpture and architecture." To his eventual regret, Roberts did not take the suggestion to Moon. As published, the text fell far short of his expectations, but he did not feel that it diminished the publication. Critics clearly agreed, for the laudatory views never mention the writing; as a vivid tale of adventurous travel, nothing rivaled Roberts's pictures.

A dedicated traveler, Roberts could not stay long in London. Within a few months of his return from the East he was again touring the highlands. He made regular trips to the continent: to Normandy and Brittany in 1843, to Belgium and Holland in 1849, and—realizing a long-delayed desire—to Italy in 1851. He took his sketchbook everywhere he went, but few subjects had the power to inspire him the way those he had found on his Eastern journey had. He wrote to Christine from France in 1843: "I have delayed writing from day to day in the hope of being able to report something favourable of my artistic tour, but with the exception of Mount St. Michael, it has hitherto been unproductive. Whether the impressions made on my mind by Egypt are never to be effaced, or whether the places I have visited here are not interesting, I have felt little inclination to do anything."

His memories of the East continued to inspire him. Almost yearly he returned to his sketchbooks to paint works for exhibition or for friends. In 1848, he painted a small, exquisite watercolor view of Dendera (Plate 6:7), allowing his artistic imagination to restore the faces of Hathor on the columns. Two years later, he returned to the subject of the simoon, in a small oil painted as a present for Charles Dickens (currently in a private collection). When the Pre-Raphaelite painter William Holman Hunt (1827–1910), who had made his own tour of the Holy Land in 1854, saw the work given to Dickens, he criticized Roberts for repositioning the Sphinx for dramatic effect. Dickens dismissed his opinions, believing that, in his "poetical conception," Roberts was allowed artistic license. Hunt was among the few to call Roberts on his practice of organizing a site for compositional advantage. More typically Roberts was praised for his unprecedented ability to render precisely what he had seen. Even John Ruskin, who dismissed the work of subsequent travel artists to the East as "the clumsiest, most vulgar, and most ludicrous pieces of work that ever disgraced draughtsmanship," found Roberts's sketches to be "faithful," produced "not to exhibit his own skill, but to give true portraiture of scenes of historical and religious interest . . . beyond any outlines from nature I had ever seen."

Within a year of Roberts's return from the East, other British artists were making journeys to the Orient. Roberts's friend John Frederick Lewis (1805–1876), who had traveled to Spain in the previous decade, went to Cairo in 1841 by way of Greece. He stayed there for more than ten years, painting scenes of exotic fantasy featuring beautiful harem girls in carefully observed and meticulously rendered architectural settings. In 1849,

Edward Lear (1812–1888) revisited most of Roberts's destinations and made his own travel views on a journey that took him from Egypt to Turkey. Roberts was influential in his friend David Wilkie's decision to go to Egypt in 1840. Wilkie even obtained an extraordinary privilege that had been denied to Roberts, a portrait sitting with Pasha Mehemet Ali (see Plate 5:14), but on his return journey, in 1841, he died of cholera in Malta. On receiving the sad news, Roberts reflected, "What a melancholy termination has Wilkie's visit to the East been, mine might have been the same." Francis Frith (1822–1898) earned the distinction of being the first photographer to document the Middle East. He made three journeys during the years 1856–1860, photographing many of the sites Roberts had drawn and extending his own expedition down the Nile to the third cataract. In some ways, Frith's work was seen to rival that of Roberts, and, when the publication of an album of his photographs was announced, the *Art Journal* exclaimed "We will *know* that we see things exactly as they are." Frith's album did impress a wide audience with the novelty and veracity associated with his medium, but by the time it appeared, in the late 1850s, Egypt and the Holy Land were no longer regarded as such alien and inaccessible destinations.

A spate of publications on the region had followed in the wake of Roberts's magisterial folios. By 1852, accounts of exotic Eastern travel had become so common that the critic for *Tait's Edinburgh Magazine* introduced a new edition of William Henry Bartlett's *Footsteps of Our Lord and His Apostles* (London: Arthur Hall, Virtue, 1851) with this exasperated observation: "Once more the east! the everlasting east! that standing dish of literary cookery, which is forever being served up, till it ceases to gratify the mental palate or

Plate 6:8 *Inauguration of the Great Exhibition: 1 May 1851.* The Royal Collection, London.

Plate 6:9 *Entrance to the North Transept, Crystal Palace,* 1851.
Oil on panel, 24 x 17 1/2 in. (61 x 44.5 cm) Royal Collection, London.

nourish the intellectual stomach. . . . Let us suppose we read, say for instance, only a few of these all but daily Oriental productions. Alas! We read them all! Yes; there they are; the same Arabs, camels, deserts, tombs and jackals that we journeyed with, rode on, traversed, dived into and cursed respectively, only a week ago, with some other traveller."

Although Roberts always regarded his Eastern journey as the pinnacle of his artistic life, he refused to let his reputation rest on old achievements. His Eastern work had brought him to the attention of Queen Victoria, and, through her influence, he received a series of official documentary commissions, including the inaugural ceremony of the Great Exhibition of 1851 (Plate 6:8) and a view of the Crystal Palace (Plate 6:9). More honorific than inspirational, these commissions were burdensome to Roberts, and his friend Lauder urged him to avoid them: "Paint no more Crystal palaces: things of that kind are unworthy of you." By the mid–1850s, contentment with his family—as well as his declining health—stilled his urge to travel. Christine's marriage to Henry Bicknell, the son of one of Roberts's closest friends and patrons, was a happy one, and this—as well as their nine children—gave Roberts unequaled joy. In 1859, a few days before his sixty-fifth birthday, he wrote to a friend, taking account of his life: "My only child is well and happy with the best of husbands, surrounded by a host of fine children. I am now enjoying the greatest of blessings, health! My foot is placed on the highest spoke of the artistic ladder and as yet without a rival in my own department. It would be strange indeed, if in my old age, with all these blessings, I did not feel happy" (Plate 6:10).

Plate 6:10 John Ballantine, *David Roberts in His Studio*, c. 1866. Fine Art Society, courtesy of Bridgeman Art Library, London.

Roberts felt that the art world had treated him well, and he demonstrated his appreciation by remaining an active and supportive member of many arts organizations, always taking a liberal stance. He strongly believed that art was not the exclusive prerogative of wealth and privilege, and he mounted several campaigns to keep the Royal Academy open on selected evenings to allow working people to see the exhibitions. He urged the establishment of national galleries throughout England and Scotland, to bring appreciation of the arts to the provinces. He was also an early advocate of architectural preservation. And, at the Royal Academy exhibition of 1859, George Eliot overheard him say: "If ever one sees a fine picture now, it is by a woman." He was always prepared to help another artist in financial trouble, ready to buy a picture or to offer a loan whether or not there was the possibility of repayment. Just as he did not forget his impoverished origins, he remembered that his own first artistic opportunities had come through the theater. On occasion, he would design scenery as a favor to a friend, often involving Stanfield or Haghe, as he did in the sets for Dickens's play *Not So Bad as We Seem* (1851). He also donated a thousand pounds to Dickens's home for "Decayed Actors," challenging Stanfield to match his generosity.

In 1860, Roberts began a new series of paintings, which he grouped under the title *Pictures of London from the Thames*. It was originally Turner's idea to paint views of London as if it were a travel destination, seen with fresh eyes and presented with enthusiastic appreciation. When Turner told Roberts of the plan, he admitted that it was too late in his own life to begin it. Nine years after the elder artist's death, Roberts took up the project, in memory of Turner. It suited the time of Roberts's life and his state of mind. It allowed him to stay near his family but satisfy his wanderlust, exploring a familiar city from a new perspective. He planned to feature all the major architectural monuments, including the new Palace at Westminster, which was nearly completed (Plate 6:11). Best of all, the project presented an excuse to take a walking tour of London, and, whenever the weather permitted, Roberts traversed the city on foot, his favorite mode of travel.

On the morning of 25 November 1864, Roberts left off working on a painting of Saint Paul's to stroll on Pall Mall. Before he reached his destination, he suffered a massive stroke. He managed to mutter his address to the crowd that gathered to help him. Carried home, he died in bed late that evening. Roberts was mourned by the art world, and the press reminded the public that he had risen to prominence from the humblest of origins. On 28 November *The Times* declared: "He belongs to that proud phalanx of men whose biographies touch most keenly all young ambition—the self-made men who from small beginnings have fought their way upwards to fame, wealth and station." But for Roberts "wealth, fame and station" had merely been the happy benefits of fulfilling the goals he had set in boyhood: to see the world and share his vision with others through his pictures. Rather than a rags-to-riches saga, Roberts's life was a traveler's tale, filled with wonderful sights and spectacles that he set before enthralled audiences, so that they felt—for a moment—that they, too, had been there.

Plate 6:11 *New Palace at Westminster from the River,* 1861. Oil, 34 x 60 in. (86.4 x 152.4 cm). Worshipful Company of Goldsmiths, London.

LIST OF ILLUSTRATIONS

Works are by David Roberts unless otherwise indicated.

CHAPTER 4.
INTERLUDE IN CAIRO

CHAPTER 5.
THE HOLY LAND

5:11   *Nazareth (General View)*. From *The Holy Land, Syria, Idumea, Arabia* (London: F. G. Moon, 1842). Library of Congress, Washington, D.C.

5:12   *Sidon (Looking towards Lebanon)*. From *The Holy Land, Syria, Idumea, Arabia* (London: F. G. Moon, 1842). Library of Congress, Washington, D.C.

5:13   *Baalbec (Remains of the Western Portico)*. From *The Holy Land, Syria, Idumea, Arabia* (London: F. G. Moon, 1842). Newberry Library, Chicago.

5:14   *Baalbec (The Doorway)*. From *The Holy Land, Syria, Idumea, Arabia* (London: F. G. Moon, 1842). Newberry Library, Chicago.

·5:15   David Wilkie, *His Highness Mehemet Ali, Pasha of Egypt*, 1841. Oil on wood. Tate Gallery, London.

5:16   *Interview with the Viceroy of Egypt at His Palace, at Alexandria*. From *Egypt and Nubia* (London: F. G. Moon, 1846–1849). Library of Congress, Washington, D.C.

CHAPTER 6.
THE RICHEST FOLIOS
THAT EVER LEFT THE EAST

6:0   *The Palace of Westminster and Whitehall Terrace*, 1862. Sotheby's, London.

6:1   David O. Hill and Robert Adamson, *Photograph of David Roberts*, c. 1843–1848. Scottish National Portrait Gallery, Edinburgh.

6:2   *Jerusalem from the Mount of Olives*, 1842. Oil on canvas. Norwich Castle Museum.

6:3   Title vignette to volume 1. From *The Holy Land, Syria, Idumea, Arabia* (London: F. G. Moon, 1842). Library of Congress, Washington, D.C.

6:4   Title vignette to volume 1. From *Egypt and Nubia* (London: F. G. Moon, 1846–1849). Library of Congress, Washington, D.C.

6:5   Title vignette to volume 2. From *Egypt and Nubia* (London: F. G. Moon, 1846–1849). Library of Congress, Washington, D.C.

6:6   C. Baugniet, *Portrait of David Roberts*, 1844. From *The Holy Land, Syria, Idumea, Arabia* (London: F. G. Moon, 1842). Library of Congress, Washington, D.C.

6:7   *Dendera*, 1848. Watercolor and bodycolor. Aberdeen Art Gallery and Museum.

6:8   *Inauguration of the Great Exhibition: 1 May 1851*. The Royal Collection, London.

6:9   *Entrance to the North Transept, Crystal Palace*, 1851. Oil on panel. Royal Collection, London.

6:10   John Ballantine, *David Roberts in His Studio*, c. 1866. Fine Art Society, courtesy of Bridgeman Art Library, London.

6:11   *New Palace at Westminster from the River*, 1861. Oil. Worshipful Company of Goldsmiths, London.

Selected Bibliography

A transcript of David Roberts's Eastern journal, copied by his daughter, Christine, is in the collection of the National Library of Scotland in Edinburgh. Only a small section of the original manuscript (7 May to 24 June 1839) survives. Roberts's correspondence with friends and family is divided among several British collections, including the National Library of Scotland, the National Art Library at the Victoria and Albert Museum in London, and the Mitchell Library in Glasgow.

The following selection of books provides an overview of Roberts's full career, travel to the Middle East in Roberts's day, and the popularity of spectacles as entertainment in Britain.

Attini, Antonio (trans. Antony Shugaar). *The Holy Land: Yesterday and Today. Lithographs and Diaries by David Roberts*. New York: Stewart, Tabori, and Chang, 1996.

Ballantine, James. *The Life of David Roberts, R.A., Compiled from His Journals and Other Sources*. Edinburgh: Adam and Charles Black, 1866.

Bendiner, Kenneth Paul. "The Portrayal of the Middle East in British Painting," Ph.D. thesis, Columbia University, 1979.

Bourbon, Fabio. *Egypt: Yesterday and Today*. New York: Stewart, Tabori, and Chang, 1996.

Bourbon, Fabio. *The Holy Land: Yesterday and Today*. New York: Stewart, Tabori, and Chang, 1996.

Chicago Public Library. *Wonders Never Ceasing! Viewmaking and the Rise of British Tourism*. Exhibit catalog. Chicago: Chicago Public Library, 1992.

Clayton, Peter A. *The Rediscovery of Ancient Egypt: Artists and Travellers in the Nineteenth Century*. London: Thames and Hudson, 1982.

Dahesh Museum. *Picturing the Middle East: A Hundred Years of European Orientalism*. Exhibit catalog. New York: Dahesh Museum, 1995.

Fagin, Brian M. *Tomb Robbers, Tourists, and Archaeologists in Egypt*. Wakefield, R.I., and London: Moyer Bell, 1992.

Fine Art Society. *Travellers: Beyond the Grand Tour*. Exhibit catalog, introduction by Lynne Thornton. London: Fine Art Society, 1980.

Godfrey, Richard T. *Printmaking in Britain: A General History from its Beginnings to the Present Day*. New York: New York University Press, 1978.

Guiterman, Helen, and Briony Llywellyn. *David Roberts*. Exhibit catalog. Oxford: Phaidon Press, 1986.

Haaften, Julia van, and Jon E. Manchip White. *Egypt and the Holy Land in Historic Photographs: 77 Views by Francis Frith*. New York: Dover Publications, 1980.

Howe, Kathleen Stewart. *Revealing the Holy Land: The Photographic Exploration of Palestine*. Exhibit catalog. Santa Barbara, Calif.: Santa Barbara Museum of Art, 1997.

Hyde, David. *Panoramania! The Art and Entertainment of the "All-Embracing" View*. Exhibit catalog. London: Trefoil Publications, for Barbican Art Gallery, 1988.

Kinnear, John G. *Cairo, Petra, and Damascus, in 1839 with Remarks on the Government of Mehemet Ali and on the Present Prospects of Syria*. London: John Murray, 1841.

Lane, Edward William. *An Account of the Manners and Customs of the Modern Egyptians*. London: Charles Knight and Co., 1836.

Manley, Deborah, ed. *The Nile: A Traveler's Anthology*. London: Cassell, 1996.

Mitchell, Timothy. *Colonising Egypt*. Berkeley: University of California Press, 1991.

National Gallery of Canada. *Egyptomania: Egypt in Western Art 1730–1930*. Exhibit catalog. Ottawa: National Gallery of Canada.

Newby, Eric, ed. *A Book of Traveler's Tales*. New York: Viking Penguin, 1987.

Redgrave, Richard, and Samuel Redgrave. *A Century of British Painters*. London: Phaidon Press, 1947.

Richardson, Robert. *Travels along the Mediterranean*. 2 vols. London: T. Cadell, 1822.

Said, Edward W. *Orientalism*. New York: Pantheon Books, 1978.

Sim, Katherine. *David Roberts, R.A., 1796–1864*. London: Quartet Books, 1984.

Twyman, Michael. *Lithography 1800–1850; The Techniques of Drawing on Stone in England and France and Their Application in Works of Topography*. London: Oxford University Press, 1970.

Wright, Thomas. *Early Travels in Palestine*. London: Henry G. Bohn, 1848.